Florida

Constitution or Form of Government for the People of

Florida

As Revised and Amended at a Convention of the People Begun and....

Florida

Constitution or Form of Government for the People of Florida
As Revised and Amended at a Convention of the People Begun and....

ISBN/EAN: 9783337102531

Printed in Europe, USA, Canada, Australia, Japan

Cover: Foto ©Suzi / pixelio.de

More available books at **www.hansebooks.com**

CONSTITUTION

OR

FORM OF GOVERNMENT

FOR THE

PEOPLE OF FLORIDA,

AS REVISED AND AMENDED

At a Convention of the People begun and holden at the
City of Tallahassee on the Third day of January,

A. D. 1861,

TOGETHER WITH THE ORDINANCES

ADOPTED BY SAID CONVENTION.

———◆◆◆———

Tallahassee:

OFFICE OF THE FLORIDIAN AND JOURNAL.

PRINTED BY DYKE & CARLISLE.

1861.

CONSTITUTION

OR

FORM OF GOVERNMENT

FOR THE

PEOPLE OF FLORIDA,

AS REVISED AND AMENDED

At a Convention of the People begun and holden at the City of Tallahassee, on the third day of January,

A. D. 1861.

————— ◆•••◆ —————

ORDINANCE OF SECESSION.

We, the People of the State of Florida, in Convention assembled, do solemnly ordain, publish and declare, that the State of Florida hereby withdraws herself from the Confederacy of States existing under the name of the United States of America, and from the existing government of said States; and that all political connection between her and the government of said States ought to be and the same is hereby totally annulled and said Union of States dissolved, and the State of Florida is hereby declared a sovereign and independent Nation; and that all ordinances heretofore adopted, in so far as they create or recognize said Union, are rescinded, and all laws or parts of laws in force in this State, in so far as they recognize or assent to said Union, be and they are hereby repealed.

Done in open Convention, January 10th, 1861.

4

ARTICLE I.

DECLARATION OF RIGHTS.

That the great and essential principles of liberty and free government may be recognized and established, we declare:

1. That all freemen, when they form a social compact, are equal, and have certain inherent and indefeasible rights, among which are those of enjoying and defending life and liberty; of acquiring, possessing, and protecting property and reputation; and of pursuing their own happiness.

2. That all political power is inherent in the people, and all free governments are founded on their authority, and established for their benefit, and therefore, they have at all times an inalienable and indefeasible right to alter or abolish their form of government, in such manner as they may deem expedient.

3 That all men have a natural and inalienable right to worship Almighty God according to the dictates of their own conscience: and that no preference shall ever be given by law to any religious establishment or mode of worship in this State.

4. That all elections shall be free and equal; and that no property qualification for eligibility to office, or for the right of suffrage,shall ever be required in this State.

5. That every citizen may freely speak, write and publish his sentiments on all subjects, being responsible for the abuse of that liberty; and no law shall ever be passed to curtail, abridge, or restrain the liberty of speech or of the press.

6. That the right of trial by jury shall forever remain inviolate.

7. That the people shall be secure in their persons, houses, papers, and possessions, from unreasonable seizures and searches: and that no warrant to search any place, or to seize any person or thing shall issue without describing the place to be searched, and the person or thing to be seized, as nearly as may be, not without probable cause, supported by oath or affirmation.

8. That no freeman shall be taken, imprisoned or disseized of his freehold, liberties, or outlawed or exiled, or in any manner destroyed or deprived of his life, liberty, or property, but by the law of the land.

9. That all Courts shall be open, and every person, for an injury done him, in his lands, goods, person or reputation, shall have remedy by due course of law; and right and justice administered without sale, denial or delay.

10. That in all criminal prosecutions, the accused hath a right to be heard by himself or counsel, or both; to demand the nature and cause of the accusation; to be confronted with the witnesses against him; to have compulsory process for obtaining witnesses in his favor; and in all prosecutions by indictment or

presentment, a speedy and public trial by an impartial jury of the county or district where the offence was committed; and shall not be compelled to give evidence against himself.

11. That all persons shall be bailable, by sufficient securities, unless in capital offences, where the proof is evident, or the presumption is strong; and the privilege of habeas corpus shall not be suspended unless, when, in case of rebellion or invasion, the public safety may require it.

12. That excessive bail shall in no case be required; nor shall excessive fines be imposed; nor shall cruel or unusual punishments be inflicted.

13. That no person shall, for the same offence, be twice put in jeopardy of life or limb.

14. That private property shall not be taken or applied to public use, unless just compensation be made therefor.

15. That in all prosecutions and indictments for libel, the truth may be given in evidence; and if it shall appear to the jury that the libel is true, and published with good motives and for justifiable ends, the truth shall be a justification: and the jury shall be the judges of the law and the facts.

16. That no person shall be put to answer any criminal charge but by presentment, indictment or impeachment.

17. That no conviction shall work corruption of blood or forfeiture of estate.

18. That retrospective laws, punishing acts committed before the existence of such laws, and by them only declared penal or criminal, are oppressive, unjust, and incompatible with liberty; wherefore, no ex post facto law shall ever be made.

19. That no law impairing the obligation of contracts shall ever be passed.

20. That the people have a right in a peaceable manner to assemble together to consult for the common good; and to apply to those invested with the powers of government, for redress of grievances, or other proper purposes, by petition, address or remonstrance.

21. That the free white men of this State shall have the right to keep and to bear arms for their common defence.

22. That no soldier in time of peace shall be quartered in any house without the consent of the owner; nor in time of war but in a manner prescribed by law.

23. That no standing army shall be kept up without the consent of the Legislature; and the military shall, in all cases and at all times, be in strict subordination to the civil power.

24. That perpetuities and monopolies are contrary to the genius of a free State, and ought not to be allowed.

25. That no hereditary emoluments, privileges or honors shall ever be granted or conferred in this State.

26. That frequent recurrence to fundamental principles is absolutely necessary to preserve the blessings of liberty.

27. That to guard against transgressions upon the rights of the people, we declare that everything in this article is excepted out of the general powers of government and shall forever remain inviolate; and that all laws contrary thereto, or to the following provisions, shall be void.

ARTICLE II.

DISTRIBUTION OF THE POWERS OF GOVERNMENT.

1. The powers of the government of the State of Florida shall be divided into three distinct departments, and each of them confided to a separate body of magistracy, to wit: those which are legislative to one; those which are Executive to another; and those which are Judicial to another.

2. No person or collection of persons, being one of those departments, shall exercise any power properly belonging to either of the others, except in the instances expressly provided for in this Constitution.

ARTICLE III.

EXECUTIVE DEPARTMENT.

1. The Supreme Executive power shall be vested in a Chief Magistrate, who shall be styled the Governor of the State of Florida.

2. The Governor shall be elected for two years, by the qualified electors, at the time and place where they shall vote for Representatives, and shall remain in office until a successor be chosen and qualified. The first election for Governor shall be held on the first Monday in October, 1865.

3. No person shall be eligible to the office of Governor unless he shall have attained the age of thirty years, and shall have been a citizen of Florida at least five years next preceding the day of election.

4. The returns of every election for Governor shall be sealed up and transmitted to the seat of government, directed to the Speaker of the House of Representatives, who shall, during the first week of the session, open and publish them in the presence of both houses of the General Assembly, and the person having the highest number of votes shall be Governor, but if two or more shall be equal and highest in votes, one of them shall be chosen Governor by the joint vote of the two houses; and contested elections for Governor shall be determined by both Houses of the General Assembly, in such manner as shall be prescribed by law.

5. He shall at stated times receive a compensation for his services, which shall not be increased or diminished during the term for which he shall have been elected.

6. He shall be Commander-in-Chief of the army and navy of this State, and of the militia thereof.

7. He may require information in writing from the officers of the Executive Departments on any subject relating to the duties of their respective offices.

8. He may, by proclamation, on extraordinary occasions, convene the General Assembly at the seat of Government, or at a different place, if that shall have become dangerous from an enemy, or from disease; and in case of disagreement between the two houses with respect to the time of adjournment, he may adjourn them to such time as he shall think proper, not beyond the day of the next meeting designated by this Constitution.

9. He shall, from time to time, give to the General Assembly information of the state of the Government, and recommend to their consideration such measures as he may deem expedient.

10. He shall take care that the laws be faithfully executed.

11. In all criminal and penal cases, (except of treason and impeachment) after conviction, he shall have power to grant reprieves and pardons, and remit fines and forfeitures, under such rules and regulations as shall be prescribed by law; and in cases of treason he shall have power, by and with the advice and consent of the Senate, to grant reprieves and pardons, and he may, in the recess of the Senate, respite the sentence until the end of the next session of the General Assembly.

12. There shall be a seal of the State, which shall be kept by the Governor, and used by him officially.

13. All commissions shall be in the name and by the authority of the State of Florida, be sealed with the State seal and signed by the Governor, and attested by the Secretary of State.

14. There shall be a Secretary of State appointed by joint vote of both Houses of the General Assembly, who shall continue in office during the term of two years; and he shall keep a fair register of the official acts and proceedings of the Governor, and shall, when required, lay the same and all papers, minutes and vouchers relative thereto, before the General Assembly, and shall perform such other duties as may be required of him by law.

15. Vacancies that happen in offices, the appointment to which is vested in the General Assembly, or given to the Governor, with the advice and consent of the Senate, shall be filled by the Governor during the recess of the General Assembly, by granting commissions, which shall expire at the end of the next session.

16. Every bill which shall have passed both Houses of the General Assembly, shall be presented to the Governor; if he approve, he shall sign it; but if not, he shall return it with his objections to the House in which it shall have originated, who shall enter the objections at large upon the journals, and proceed to reconsider it; and if after such reconsideration two-thirds of the whole number elected to that House shall agree to pass the bill, it shall be sent with the objections to the other House, by which it shall likewise be reconsidered; and if approved by two-thirds of the whole number elected to that House, it shall become a law; but in such cases, the votes of both Houses shall be by yeas and nays, and the names of the members voting for or against the bill, shall be entered on the journals of each House respectively; and if any bill shall not be returned by the Governor within five days (Sundays excepted) after it shall have been presented to him, the same shall be a law in like manner as if he had signed it, unless the General Assembly, by their adjournment, prevent its return, in which case it shall not be a law.

17. Every order, resolution or vote, to which concurrence of both Houses may be necessary, except on questions of adjournment, shall be presented to the Governor, and before it shall take effect, be approved by him, or being disapproved, be re-passed by both Houses, according to the rules and limitations prescribed in case of a bill.

18. In case of the impeachment of the Governor, his removal from office, death, refusal to qualify, resignation, or absence from the State, the President of the Senate shall exercise all the power and authority appertaining to the office of Governor, during the term for which the Governor was elected, unless the General Assembly shall provide by law for the election of a Governor to fill such vacancy; or, until the Governor absent, or impeached, shall return or be acquitted.

19. If, during the vacancy of the office of Governor, the President of the Senate shall be impeached, removed from office, refuse to qualify, resign, die or be absent from the State, the Speaker of the House of Representatives shall in like manner administer the Government.

20. The President of the Senate or Speaker of the House of Representatives, during the time he administers the government, shall receive the same compensation which the Governor would have received.

21. It shall be the duty of the General Assembly to provide for the purchase or erection of a suitable building for the residence of the Governor; and the Governor shall reside at the seat of government. But whenever by reason of danger from an enemy, or from disease, the Governor may deem the capital un-

safe, he may by proclamation fix the seat of government at some secure place within the State, until such danger cease.

22. No person shall hold the office of Governor and any other office or commission, civil or military, either in this State, or under the Confederate States, or any other power, at one and the same time, except the President of the Senate, or the Speaker of the House of Representatives, when he shall hold the office as aforesaid.

23. A State Treasurer and Comptroller of Public Accounts shall be elected every two years by joint vote of both Houses of the General Assembly.

ARTICLE IV.

LEGISLATIVE DEPARTMENT.

1. The Legislative power of this State shall be vested in two distinct branches, the one to be styled the Senate, the other the House of Representatives, and both together the "General Assembly of the State of Florida," and the style of all the laws shall be, "Be it enacted by the Senate and House of Representatives of the State of Florida in General Assembly convened."

2. The members of the House of Representatives shall be chosen by the qualified voters, and shall serve for the term of two years from and after the day of the first election under this amended Constitution, and no longer; and the sessions of the General Assembly shall be annual, and commence on the third Monday in November in each year, or at such other times as may be prescribed by law.

3. The Representatives shall be chosen on the first Monday in October, each and every second year, from and after the first election under this amended Constitution, or on such other day as may be directed by law.

4. The first election for Assemblymen under this Constitution, shall take place on the first Monday in October, eighteen hundred and sixty-two; and the first session of the General Assembly, under this amended Constitution, shall commence on the third Monday in November, in the year eighteen hundred and sixty-two.

5. No person shall be a Representative unless he be a white man, a citizen of the Confederate States of America, and shall have been an inhabitant of the State two years next preceding his election, and the last year thereof a resident of the county for which he shall be chosen, and shall have attained the age of twenty-one years.

6. The Senators shall be chosen by the qualified electors for the term of four years, at the same time, in the same manner, and in the same places where they vote for members of the House

of Representatives; and no man shall be a Senator unless he be a white man, a citizen of the Confederate States, and shall have been an inhabitant of this State two years next preceding his election, and the last year thereof a resident of the district or county for which he shall be chosen, and shall have attained the age of twenty-five years.

7. The House of Representatives, when assembled, shall choose a Speaker and its other officers, and each House shall be judge of the qualifications, elections and returns of its members; but a contested election shall be determined in such manner as shall be directed by law.

8. A majority of each House shall constitute a quorum to do business, but a smaller number may adjourn from day to day, and may compel the attendance of absent members, in such manner and under such penalties as each House may prescribe.

9. Each House may determine the rules of its own proceedings, punish its members for disorderly behavior, and, with the consent of two-thirds, expel a member, but not a second time for the same cause.

10. Each House, during the session, may punish by imprisonment any person not a member, for disrespectful or disorderly behavior in its presence, or for obstructing any of its proceedings, provided such imprisonment shall not extend beyond the end of the session.

11. Each House shall keep a journal of its proceedings, and cause the same to be published immediately after its adjournment; and the yeas and nays of the members of each House shall be taken and entered upon the journals upon the final passage of every bill, and may, by any two members, be required upon any other question; and any member of either House shall have liberty to dissent from or protest against any act or resolution which he may think injurious to the public or an individual, and have the reasons of his dissent entered on the journal.

12. Senators and Representatives shall, in all cases, except treason, felony or breach of the peace, be privileged from arrest during the session of the General Assembly, and in going to or returning from the same, allowing one day for every twenty miles such member may reside from the place at which the General Assembly is convened; and for any speech or debate in either House, they shall not be questioned in any other place.

13. The General Assembly shall make provision by law for filling vacancies that may occur in either House by the death, resignation (or otherwise) of any of its members.

14. The doors of each House shall be open, except on such occasions as in the opinion of the House the public safety may imperiously require secrecy.

15. Neither House shall, without the consent of the other,

adjourn for more than three days, nor to any other place than that in which they may be sitting.

16. Bills may originate in either House of the General Assembly, and all bills passed by one House may be discussed, amended or rejected by the other; but no bill shall have the force of law until on three several days it be read in each House and free discussion be allowed thereon, unless, in cases of urgency, four-fifths of the House in which the same shall be depending, may deem it expedient to dispense with the rule; and every bill having passed both Houses, shall be signed by the Speaker and President of their respective Houses.

17. Each member of the General Assembly shall receive from the public treasury such compensation for his services as may be fixed by law, but no increase of compensation shall take effect during the term for which the Representatives were elected when such law was passed.

18. The number of members of the House of Representatives shall never exceed sixty.

19. The sessions of the General Assembly shall not extend in duration over thirty days, unless it be deemed expedient by a concurrent majority of two-thirds of the members of each House, and no member shall receive pay from the State for his services after the expiration of sixty days continuously from the commencement of the session.

20. The General Assembly may by law authorize the Circuit Court to grant licenses for building toll-bridges and to establish ferries, and to regulate the tolls of both, to construct dams across streams not navigable, to ascertain and declare what streams are navigable; but no special law for such purpose shall be made.

21. The General Assembly shall pass a *general* law prescribing the manner in which names of persons may be changed, but no special law for such purpose shall be passed; and no law shall be made allowing married women or minors to contract or to manage their estates, or to legitimate bastards.

22. The General Assembly shall have power to tax the lands and slaves of non-residents higher than the like property of residents.

23. The public lands accruing to the State in consequence of the dissolution of the late Union between Florida and the United States, shall be applied exclusively to the payment of the debt and necessary expenses of the State, and no law shall be passed granting such lands for any other purpose.

24. The General Assembly shall pass a *general* law for the incorporation of towns, religious, literary, scientific, benevolent, military and other associations, not commercial, industrial or financial, but no *special* act incorporating any such associations, shall be passed.

25. No act incorporating any railroad, banking, insurance, commercial, industrial, or financial corporation, shall be introduced into the General Assembly, unless the person or persons applying for such incorporation shall have deposited with the Treasurer the sum of one hundred dollars as a bonus to the State.

26. Officers shall be removed from office for incapacity, misconduct, or neglect of duty; and where no special mode of trial is provided by the Constitution, the General Assembly shall pass a law providing the mode in which such trials shall be had, which shall be before a jury and in the Circuit Court.

27. The General Assembly shall have power to create special tribunals for the trial of offences committed by slaves, free negroes and mulattoes; and until the General Assembly otherwise provides, there is hereby created a Court in each county, which shall consist of two Justices of the Peace, and twelve citizens, being qualified Jurors of the county, who shall have power to try all cases of felony committed in their county by slaves, free negroes and mulattoes. A majority of said Court may pronounce judgment, and all trials before it shall be had upon the statement of the offence in the warrant of arrest, and without presentment or indictment by a Grand Jury. The Sheriff of the county shall act as the ministerial officer of said Court, and the citizens who, with the Justices, are to compose the same, shall be selected by said Justices and summoned to attend by the Sheriff; and appeals from the judgment of said Court shall be had to the Circuit Court of the county upon an order made by the Judge thereof, upon an inspection of the record of the trial, full minutes of which shall be made by the said Justices, and such appeal, when allowed, shall operate as a supersedeas of the judgment.

ARTICLE V.

JUDICIAL DEPARTMENT.

1. The Judicial power of this State, both as to matters of law and equity, shall be vested in a Supreme Court, Courts of Chancery, Circuit Courts and Justices of the Peace, provided the General Assembly may also vest such criminal jurisdiction as may be deemed necessary in corporation Courts; but such jurisdiction shall not extend to capital offences.

2. The Supreme Court, except in cases otherwise directed in this Constitution, shall have appellate jurisdiction only, which shall be co-extensive with the State, under such restrictions and regulations, not repugnant to this Constitution, as may from time to time be prescribed by law, provided that the said Court shall always have power to issue writs of injunction, mandamus, quo warranto, habeas corpus, and such other remedial and original

writs as may be necessary to give it a general superintendence and control of all other Courts.

3. The Supreme Court, when organized, shall be holden at such times and places as may be provided by law.

4. The State shall be divided into convenient Circuits; and for each Circuit there shall be a Judge, who shall, after his election or appointment, reside in the Circuit for which he has been elected or appointed, and shall at stated times receive for his services a salary of not less than two thousand dollars per annum, which shall not be diminished during the continuance of such judge in office; but the judges shall receive no fees or perquisites of office, nor hold any other office of profit under the State, the Confederate States, or any other power.

5. The Circuit Courts shall have original jurisdiction in all matters, civil and criminal, within this State, not otherwise excepted in this Constitution.

6. A Circuit Court shall be held in such counties and at such times and places therein as may be prescribed by law, and the judges of the several Circuit Courts may hold courts for each other, and shall do so when directed by law.

7. The General Assembly shall have power to establish and organize a separate Court or Courts of original Equity jurisdiction; but until such Court or Courts shall be established and organized, the Circuit Courts shall exercise such jurisdiction.

8. The General Assembly shall provide by law for the appointment in each County of an officer to take probate of wills, to grant letters testamentary, of administration and guardianship, to attend to the settlement of the estates of decedents, and of minors, and to discharge the duties usually appertaining to courts of ordinary, subject to the direction and supervision of the Courts of Chancery, as may be provided by law.

9. A competent number of Justices of the Peace shall be, from time to time, appointed or elected, in and for each County, in such mode and for such term of office as the General Assembly may direct, and shall possess such jurisdiction as may be prescribed by law; and in cases tried before a Justice of the Peace, the right of appeal shall be secured, under such rules and regulations as may be prescribed by law.

10. Judges of the Supreme Court, Chancellors, and Judges of the Circuit Court, shall be appointed by the Governor, by and with the advice and consent of two-thirds of the Senate, when in session, and hold office for the term of six years from the date of their appointment, unless sooner removed under the provisions made in this Constitution for the removal of Judges by address or impeachment; and for wilful neglect of duty or other reasonable cause, which shall not be sufficient ground for impeachment, the Governor shall remove any of them on the address of two-

thirds of the General Assembly : *Provided, however,* That the cause or causes shall be stated at length in such address, and entered on the journals of each House : *And provided further.* That the cause or causes shall be notified to the Judge so intended to be removed, and he shall be admitted to a hearing in his own defence before any vote for such removal shall pass, and in such cases the vote shall be taken by yeas and nays and entered on the journals of each House respectively.

11. Whenever the General Assembly shall create a separate Chancery Court, under the provisions of this Constitution, the Judges thereof shall be elected in the manner provided in the 10th clause of this article, and shall hold their offices for the same term, and be subject to all the provisions of said clause.

12. The Clerk of the Supreme Court, and the Clerks of the Courts of Chancery shall be appointed by the Judges of their respective Courts; and the Clerks of the Circuit Courts shall be elected by the qualified electors, in such mode as may be prescribed by law.

13. The Justices of the Supreme Court, Chancellors and Judges of the Circuit Courts, shall, by virtue of their offices, be conservators of the peace throughout the State, and Justices of the Peace in their respective counties.

14. The style of all process shall be "The State of Florida," and all criminal prosecutions shall be carried on in the name of the State of Florida, and all indictments shall conclude, "against the peace and dignity of the same."

15. There shall be an Attorney General for the State, who shall reside at the seat of Government. It shall be his duty to attend all sessions of the General Assembly, and upon the passage of any act, to draft and submit to the General Assembly, at the same session, all necessary forms of proceedings under such laws, which, when approved, shall be published therewith ; and he shall perform such other duties as may be prescribed by law. He shall be elected by joint vote of the two Houses of the General Assembly, and shall hold his office for two years, but may be removed by the Governor on the address of two-thirds of the two Houses of the General Assembly, and shall receive for his services a compensation to be fixed by law.

16. There shall be one Solicitor for each Circuit, who shall reside therein and shall be elected by the qualified voters of such Circuit, on the first Monday in October in the year one thousand eight hundred and sixty-one, and every four years thereafter, or at such time as the General Assembly may by law prescribe, and he shall receive for his services a compensation to be fixed by law.

17. No Justice of the Supreme Court shall sit as Judge or take

part in the appellate Court on the trial or hearing of any case which shall have been decided by him in the Court below.

18. The General Assembly shall have power to establish in each county a Board of Commissioners for the regulation of the county business therein.

19. No duty, not judicial, shall be imposed by law upon the Justices of the Supreme Court, Chancellors, or the Judges of the Circuit Courts, of this State.

ARTICLE VI.

THE RIGHT OF SUFFRAGE AND QUALIFICATIONS OF OFFICERS; CIVIL. OFFICERS, AND IMPEACHMENTS AND REMOVALS FROM OFFICE.

1. Every free white male person of the age of twenty-one years and upwards, and who shall be at the time of offering to vote, a citizen of the Confederate States, and who shall have resided and had his habitation, domicil, home and place of permanent abode in Florida for one year next preceding the election at which he shall offer to vote, and who shall have at such time and for six months immediately preceding said time, shall have had his habitation, domicil, home and place of permanent abode in the county in which he may offer to vote, and shall have paid all taxes due by him at least five days before the day of election, shall be deemed a qualified elector at all elections under this Constitution, and none others shall be, except in elections by general ticket in the State or District prescribed by law, in which cases the elector must have been a resident of the State one year next preceding the election, and six months within the election district in which he offers to vote: *Provided*, That no person in the regular army or navy of the Confederate States, unless he be a qualified elector of the State previous to his entry in the regular army or navy of the Confederate States, or of the revenue service, shall be considered a resident of the State in consequence of being stationed within the same.

2. The General Assembly shall have power to exclude from every office of honor, trust or profit within the State, and from the right of suffrage, all persons convicted of bribery, perjury or other infamous crime.

3. No person shall be capable of holding or being elected to any post of honor, profit, trust or emolument, civil or military, legislative, executive or judicial, under the government of this State, who shall hereafter fight a duel or send or accept a challenge to fight a duel, the probable issue of which may be the death of the challenger or challenged, or who shall be a second to either party, or who shall in any manner aid or assist in such duel, or shall be knowingly the bearer of such challenge or acceptance, whether the same occur or be committed in or out of

the State; but the legal disability shall not accrue until after trial and conviction, according to due form of law.

4. No person who may hereafter be a collector or holder of public moneys shall have a seat in either House of the General Assembly, or be eligible to any office of trust or profit under this State, until he shall have accounted for and paid into the treasury all sums for which he may be accountable.

5. No Governor, member of Congress or of the General Assembly of this State, shall receive a fee, be engaged as counsel, agent or attorney in any civil case or claim against this State, or to which this State shall be a party, during the time he shall remain in office.

6. No Senator or Representative shall, during the term for which he shall have been elected, be appointed to any civil office of profit under this State which shall have been created, or the emoluments of which shall have been increased during such term, except such offices as may be filled by elections by the people.

7. Members of the General Assembly and all officers, civil or military, before they enter upon the execution of their respective offices, shall take the following oath or affirmation: I do swear (or affirm) that I am duly qualified, according to the Constitution of this State, to exercise the office to which I have been elected (or appointed,) and will, to the best of my abilities discharge the duties thereof, and preserve, protect and defend the Constitution of this State, and of the Confederate States of America.

8. Every person shall be disqualified from serving as Governor, Senator, Representative, or from holding any other office of honor or profit in this State, for the term for which he shall have been elected, who shall have been convicted of having given or offered any bribe to procure his election.

9. Laws shall be made by the General Assembly to exclude from office and from suffrage those who shall have been or may hereafter be convicted of bribery, perjury, forgery, or other high crime or misdemeanor; and the privilege of suffrage shall be supported by laws regulating elections and prohibiting under adequate penalties, all undue influence thereon, from power, bribery, tumult, or other improper practices.

10. All civil officers of the State at large shall reside within the State, and all district or county officers within their respective districts or counties, and shall keep their respective offices at such places therein as may be required by law.

11. It shall be the duty of the General Assembly to regulate by law in what cases, and what deduction from the salaries of public officers shall be made for neglect of duty in their official capacity.

12. Returns of elections for members of Congress and the General Assembly, shall be made to the Secretary of State, in manner to be prescribed by law.

13. In all elections by the General Assembly the vote shall be *viva voce*, and in all elections by the people the vote shall be by ballot.

14. No member of Congress or person holding or exercising any office of profit under the Confederate States, or under any foreign power, shall be eligible as a member of the General Assembly of this State, or hold, or exercise any office of profit under the State; and no person in this State shall ever hold two offices of profit at the same time, except the office of Justice of the Peace, Notary Public, Constable and Militia offices.

15. The General Assembly shall, by law, provide for the appointment or election and the removal from office of all officers, civil and military, in this State, not provided for in this Constitution.

16. The power of impeachment shall be vested in the House of Representatives.

17. All impeachments shall be tried by the Senate, and, when sitting for that purpose, the Senators shall be upon oath or affirmation, and no person shall be convicted without the concurrence of two-thirds of the members present.

18. The Governor and all civil officers shall be liable to impeachment for any misdemeanor in office; but judgment in such cases shall not extend further than to removal from office and disqualification to hold any office of honor, trust or profit under this State: but the parties shall nevertheless be liable to indictment, trial and punishment, according to law.

ARTICLE VII.

MILITIA.

1. All militia officers shall be elected or appointed under such rules and regulations as the General Assembly may from time to time direct and establish.

2. All offences against the militia laws shall be tried by Court Martial or before a court and jury, as the General Assembly may direct.

3. No commission shall be vacated except by sentence of Court Martial.

ARTICLE VIII.

TAXATION AND REVENUE.

1. The General Assembly shall devise and adopt a system of revenue, having regard to an equal and uniform mode of taxation to be general throughout the State.

2

. 2. No other or greater amount of tax or revenue shall at any time be levied, than may be required for the necessary expenses of government.

3. No money shall be drawn from the Treasury but in consequence of an appropriation by law, and a regular statement of the receipts and the expenditures of all public monies shall be published and promulgated annually with the laws of the General Assembly.

4. The General Assembly shall have power to authorize the several counties and incorporated towns in this State to impose taxes for county and corporation purposes, respectively, and all property shall be taxed upon the principles established in regard to State taxation.

ARTICLE IX.

CENSUS AND APPORTIONMENT OF REPRESENTATION.

1. The General Assembly shall, in the year one thousand eight hundred and sixty-five, and every tenth year thereafter, cause an enumeration to be made of all the inhabitants of the State, and to the whole number of free white inhabitants shall be added three-fifths of the number of slaves, and they shall then proceed to apportion the representation equally among the different counties, according to such enumeration, giving, however, one representative to every county, and increasing the number of representatives on a uniform ratio of population, according to the foregoing basis, and which ratio shall not be changed until a new census shall have been taken.

2. The General Assembly shall also, after every such enumeration, proceed to fix by law the number of Senators which shall constitute the Senate of the State of Florida, and which shall never be less than one-fourth, nor more than one half of the whole number of the House of Representatives; and they shall lay off the State into the same number of senatorial districts, as nearly equal in the number of inhabitants as may be, according to the ratio of representation established in the preceding section, each of which districts shall be entitled to one Senator.

3. When any senatorial district shall be composed of two or more counties, the counties of which such district consists shall not be entirely separated by any county belonging to another district, and no county shall be divided in forming a district.

4. No county now organized shall be divided into new counties so as to reduce the inhabitants of either below the ratio of representation.

ARTICLE X.

EDUCATION.

1. The proceeds of all lands that have been granted by the United States for the use of Schools and a Seminary or Seminaries of Learning, shall be and remain a perpetual fund, the interest of which, together with all moneys derived from any other source, applicable to the same object, shall be inviolably appropriated to the use of Schools and Seminaries of Learning respectively, and to no other purpose.

2. The General Assembly shall take such measures as may be necessary to preserve, from waste or damage, all land so granted and appropriated to the purposes of Education.

ARTICLE XI.

PUBLIC DOMAIN AND INTERNAL IMPROVEMENTS.

1. It shall be the duty of the General Assembly to provide for the prevention of waste and damage of the public lands, now possessed or that may hereafter be ceded to the State of Florida, and it may pass laws for the sale of any part or portion thereof, and in such case provide for the safety, security and appropriation of the proceeds.

2. A liberal system of Internal Improvements being essential to the development of the resources of the country, shall be encouraged by the government of this State; and it shall be the duty of the General Assembly, as soon as practicable, to ascertain by law proper objects of improvement in relation to roads, canals and navigable streams, and to provide for a suitable application of such funds as may be appropriated for such improvements.

ARTICLE XII.

BOUNDARIES.

1. The jurisdiction of the State of Florida shall extend over the Territories of East and West Florida, which, by the treaty of amity, settlement and limits between the United States and his Catholic Majesty, on the 22d day of February, A. D. 1819, were ceded to the United States.

ARTICLE XIII.

BANKS AND OTHER CORPORATIONS.

1. The General Assembly shall pass no act of incorporation or make any alteration therein unless with the assent of at least two-

thirds of each house, and unless public notice, in one or more newspapers in the State, shall have been given, for at least three months immediately preceding the session at which the same may be applied for.

2. No banking corporation shall be created or continue, which is composed of a less number than twenty individuals, a majority of whom at least shall be residents of the State; and no other corporation shall be created or continue composed of a less number than ten, of whom at least five shall be residents of this State.

3. No bank charter or any act of incorporation granting exclusive privileges, shall be granted for a longer period than twenty years.

4. The charters of banks granted by the General Assembly shall restrict such banks to the business of exchange, discount and deposite; and they shall not speculate or deal in real estate or the stock of other corporations or associations, or in any merchandise or chattels, or be concerned in insurance, manufacturing, exportation or importation, except of bullion or specie; shall not act as trustee in anywise, nor shall they own real estate or chattels, except such as shall be necessary for their actual use in the transaction of business, or which may be pledged as further security or received towards or in satisfaction of previously contracted debts, or purchased at legal sales to satisfy such debts, of which they shall be required to make sale within two years after the acquisition thereof.

5. The capital stock of any bank shall not be less than one hundred thousand dollars, and shall be created only by the actual payment of specie therein; and no bank shall borrow money to create or add to its capital or to conduct its business, and no loans shall be made on stock.

6. All liabilities of such banks shall be payable in specie. The aggregate of the liabilities and issues of a bank, exclusive of deposits, shall at no time exceed double the amount of its capital stock paid in.

7. No dividends of profits exceeding ten per centum per annum on the capital stock paid in shall be made, but all profits over ten per centum per annum shall be set apart and retained as a safety fund.

8. Stockholders in a bank, when an act of forfeiture of its charter is committed, or when it is dissolved or expires, shall be individually and severally liable for the payment of all its debts, in proportion to the stock owned by each.

9. Banks shall be open to inspection, under such regulations as may be prescribed by law, and it shall be the duty of the Governor to appoint a person or persons, not connected in any manner with any bank in the State, to examine at least once a year into

their state and condition; and the officers of every bank shall make quarterly returns to the Governor of its state and condition, and the names of the stockholders and shares held by each.

10. *Non user* for the space of one year, or any act of a corporation, or those having the control or management thereof, or intrusted therewith, inconsistent with or in violation of the provisions of this constitution, or of its charter, shall cause its forfeiture, and the General Assembly shall by general law provide a summary process for the sequestration of its effects and assets, the appointment of officers to settle its affairs, and no forfeited charter shall be restored. The foregoing provisions shall not be construed to prevent the General Assembly from imposing other restrictions and provisions in the creation of corporations.

11. The General Assembly shall not pledge the faith and credit of the State to raise funds in aid of any corporation whatever. .

ARTICLE XIV.

AMENDMENTS AND REVISIONS OF THE CONSTITUTION.

1. No part of this Constitution shall be altered except by a Convention duly elected.

2. No Convention of the people shall be called unless by the concurrence of two-thirds of all the members of each House of the General Assembly, made known by the passing of a bill which shall be read three times on three several days in each House.

3. Whenever a Convention shall be called, proclamation of an election for delegates shall be made by the Governor at least thirty days before the day of election. Every County and Senatorial District shall be entitled to as many delegates as it has representatives in the Assembly. The same qualifications shall be required in delegates and in electors that are required in members of Assembly and voters for the same respectively, and the elections for delegates to a Convention, and the returns of such elections, shall be held and made in the manner prescribed by law for regulating elections for members of Assembly, but the Convention shall judge of the qualifications of its members.

ARTICLE XV.

GENERAL PROVISIONS.

1. The General Assembly shall have no power to pass laws for the emancipation of slaves.

2. The General Assembly shall have power to pass laws to prevent free negroes, mulattoes, and other persons of color from immigrating to this State, or from being discharged from on board any vessel in any of the ports of Florida.

3. Treason against the State shall consist only in levying war

against it or in adhering to its enemies, giving them aid and comfort. No person shall be convicted of treason unless on the testimony of two witnesses to the same overt act, or his confession in open court.

4. Divorces from the bonds of matrimony shall not be allowed but by the judgment of a court, as shall be prescribed by law.

5. The General Assembly shall declare by law what parts of the common law, and what parts of the civil law, not inconsistent with this Constitution, shall be in force in this State.

6. The oaths of officers directed to be taken under this Constitution, may be administered by any Judge or Justice of the Peace of the State of Florida, until otherwise prescribed by law.

7. The Courts of this State shall never entertain jurisdiction of any grants of land, in the Floridas, made by the King of Spain, or by his authority, subsequent to the twenty-fourth day of January, eighteen hundred and eighteen, nor shall the said Courts receive as evidence, in any case, certain grants said to have been made by the said King of Spain in favor of the Duke of Alagon, the Count Punon Rostro, and Don Pedro de Vargas, or any title derived from either of said Grants.

—•◄••►•—

Done in Convention, of the People of Florida, on the 27th day of April, one thousand eight hundred and sixty-one, at the Capitol, at Tallahassee.

JOHN C. McGEHEE, *President.*

DELEGATES:

S. S. ALDERMAN,
A. K. ALLISON,
J. PATTON ANDERSON,
S. J. BAKER,
J. L. G. BAKER,
E. P. BARRINGTON,
JOHN BEARD,
WINER BETHEL,
JAS. H. CHANDLER,
JOSEPH A. COLLIER,
ISAAC S. COON,
JAS. G. COOPER,
J. M. DANIEL,
W. G. M. DAVIS,
JAS. B. DAWKINS,
J. O. DEVALL,
W. S. DILWORTH,
JOSEPH FINEGAN,
L. A. FOLSOM,
S. M. G. GARY,
JAMES GETTIS,
EZEKIEL GLAZIER,
R. R. GOLDEN,
WM. T. GREGORY,
GEORGE HELVENSTON,
S. J. HENDRICKS,
THOS. Y. HENRY,
GREEN H. HUNTER,
F. B. IRWIN,
JOHN W. JONES,
JAMES KIRKSEY,
DANIEL LADD,
THOMPSON B. LAMAR,
JOHN J. LAMB,
A. J. LEA,

DAVID G. LEIGH,
DAVID LEWIS,
E. C. LOVE,
A. L. McCASKILL,
W. McGAHAGIN,
D. D. McLEAN,
McQUEEN McINTOSH,
ADAM McNEALEY,
R. G. MAYS,
JOHN MORRISON,
JACKSON MORTON,
JAS. A. NEWMAN,
A. W. NICHOLSON,
JAS. B. OWENS,
THOS. M. PALMER,
GEO. W. PARKHILL,
JOHN C. PELOT,
WM. PINKNEY,
ISAAC N. RUTLAND,
J. P. SANDERSON,
B. W. SAXON,*
WM. H. SEVER,
S. W. SPENCER,
E. E. SIMPSON,
MATHEW SOLANA,
SAMUEL B. STEPHENS,
JOS. M. TAYLOR,†
JAMES THOMAS,
ASA F. TIFT,
SIMON TURMAN,
GEO. T. WARD,
WM. W. WOODRUFF,
S. H. WRIGHT,
N. B. YATES.

Attest—WM. S. HARRIS, *Secretary of Convention.*

*Died during the first Session.   †Elected vice Saxon, deceased.

ORDINANCES.

●

[No. 23.]

Be it ordained by the people of the State of Florida in Convention assembled, That the legal disability, under the 5th section of the 6th article of the Constitution, shall not accrue until after trial and conviction, according to due form of law.

Be it further ordained, That the tenth section of the sixth article of the Constitution be and the same is hereby abrogated and annulled.

Done in open Convention, February, 28th, 1861.

·| No. 24. |

Be it ordained by the people of the State of Florida in Convention assembled, That whereas, an act passed by the General Assembly at its last session, entitled " An Act to prevent the collection of debts in certain cases from debtors in this State," is inconsistent with the ninth and nineteenth sections of the first article of the Constitution of this State, the said act be and the same is hereby annulled.

Done in open Convention, February, 28th 1861.

| No. 25. |

Be it ordained by the people of the State of Florida in Convention assembled, That the Constitution for the Provisional Government of the Confederate States of America, recently adopted by delegates from the States of States of South Carolina, Georgia, Alabama, Mississippi, Louisiana and Florida, assembled in Congress at the city of Montgomery, be and the same is hereby ratified and confirmed, and made the supreme law of the State of Florida, until such time as a permanent Constitution for the Government of said Confederate States shall have been adopted, and to its maintenance and support "we pledge our lives, our fortunes, and our sacred honors."

Done in open Convention, February 28th, 1861.

[No. 26.]

An Ordinance to amend the 14th Article of the Constitution.

Be it ordained by the people of the State of Florida in Convention assembled, That the 14th Article of the Constitution be and the same is hereby altered and amended, so as to read as follows:

Amendments and revisions of the Constitution.

ARTICLE XIV.

SEC. 1. No part of this Constitution shall be altered, except by a Convention duly elected.

SEC. 2. No Convention of the People shall be called, unless by the concurrence of two-thirds of all the members of each House of the General Assembly, made known by the passing of a bill, which shall be read three times on three several days in each House.

SEC. 3. Whenever a Convention shall be called, proclamation of an election for Delegates shall be made by the Governor, at least thirty days before the day of election. Every County and Senatorial District shall be entitled to as many delegates as it has representrtives in the Assembly; the same qualifications shall be required in Delegates and in Electors that are required in members of Assembly, and voters for the same respectively, and the election for Delegates to a Convention, and the returns of such elections, shall be held and made in the manner prescribed by law for regulating elections for members of Assembly; but the Convention shall judge of the qualifications of its members.

Done in open Convention March 1st, 1861.

[No. 27.]

Be it ordained by the people of the State of Florida in Convention assembled, That the General Assembly shall have power to create special tribunals for the trial of offences committed by slaves, free negroes, and mulattoes; and until the General Assembly otherwise provides, there is hereby created a court in each county, which shall consist of two Justices of the Peace and twelve citizens, being slaveholders of the county, who shall have power to try all cases of felony committed in their county by slaves, free negroes, and mulattoes a majority of said court may pronounce judgment, and all trials before it shall be had upon the statement of the offence in the warrant of arrest, and without presentment or indictment by a Grand Jury; the Sheriff of the county shall act as the ministerial officer of said court; and the citizens, who with the Justices are to compose the same, shall be selected by said Justices and summoned to attend by the Sheriff; and said court shall assess the value of all slaves sentenced by it to capital punishment, one-half of which value shall be paid by the State to the owner or owners of such slave; and appeals from the judgment of said court shall be had to the Circuit Court of the county, upon an order made by the Judge thereof, upon an inspection of the record of the trial, full minutes of which shall be made by the said Justices, and such appeal, when allowed, shall operate as a *supersedeas* of the judgment.

Passed in open Convention, Friday, April 19th, 1861.

{ No. 28. }

Ordinance of Ratification.

WHEREAS, By act of the General Assembly of the State of Florida, a Convention of the people was ordained to be assembled in the city of Tallahassee, on the 3d day of January, A. D. 1861, "for the purpose of taking into consideration the dangers incident to the position of this State in the Federal Union, and the measures which may be necessary and proper for providing against the same, and to amend the Constitution of the State of Florida so far as the same, in the judgment of said Convention, may be necessary, and thereupon to take care that the Commonwealth of Florida shall suffer no detriment;

And whereas, We the delegates of the people of the State of Florida did, in pursuance of said act, assemble in Convention on the day and in the place therein specified, and being thus charged with the duties aforesaid, after mature deliberation, and in considerate performance thereof, did, on the 10th day of January, in the year of our Lord one thousand eight hundred and sixty-one, in Convention as aforesaid, ordain publish and declare "That the State of Florida hereby withdraws herself from the Confederacy of States, existing under the name of the United States of America, and from the existing Government of said States, and that all political connection between her and the Government of said States ought to be and the same is hereby totally annulled, and said Union of States dissolved, and the State of Florida declared a sovereign and independent Nation: and that all ordinances heretofore adopted, in so far as they create or recognize said Union, are rescinded, and all laws or parts of laws in force in this State, in so far as they recognize or assent to said Union, be and they are hereby repealed;"

And whereas, The people of the State of South Carolina, in Convention assembled, had dissolved their connection with the Government of the United States of America, and invited such other of the slaveholding States, as might, in like manner declare their independence, to meet her in Convention at Montgomery, in the State of Alabama, for the purpose of forming a new Government;

And whereas, This Convention did appoint three delegates to meet in a Convention of States at Montgomery aforesaid, on the 13th day of February last, or at such other time and place as might be agreed upon, the delegates of such other slaveholding States, as then had or should have, before the final adjournment of said Convention dissolved their connection with the late Federal Union, for the purpose, among other things, of forming a "Permanent Government" for a Confederacy of such States:

And whereas, A Convention of delegates from the following States, viz: South Carolina, Georgia, Florida, Alabama, Mississipi, Louisiana and Texas, met at Montgomery aforesaid, and on the eleventh day of March, Anno Domini 1861, agreed upon and reported to the Convention of the several States, therein represented, a Constitution for the Confederate States of America;

Now be it known, That we, the delegates, of the people of the State of Florida in Convention assembled, in the name and in behalf of the people the State, having maturely deliberated and fully considered the aforesaid proposed Constitution, do by these presents, assent to and ratify the Constitution adopted by the Congress of States aforesaid, on the 11th day of March.

Anno Domini 1861, at Montgomery, in the State of Alabama, for the Government of the Confederate States of America; *Declaring, nevertheless,* That as the powers conferred through said Constitution on the Confederate Government emanate from the people of the several States in their separate sovereign capacity, said powers may be resumed in the same manner in which they are delegated, whenever they shall be perverted to the injury of the people, each State, by her delegates in Convention, having the right to judge of the occasion that may require such action ; and hereby announcing to all those whom it may concern that the said Constitution is binding on the people of the State of Florida, according to an authentic copy hereto annexed, in the words following, viz:

CONSTITUTION OF THE CONFEDERATE STATES OF AMERICA.

We, the people of the Confederate States, each State acting in its sovereign and independent character, in order to form a permanent Federal Government, establish justice, insure domestic tranquility, and secure the blessings of liberty to ourselves and our posterity—invoking the favor and guidance of Almighty God—do ordain and establish this Constitution for the Confederate States of America.

ARTICLE I.

SECTION 1.

All legislative powers herein delegated shall be vested in a Congress of the Confederate States, which shall consist of a Senate and House of Representatives.

SECTION 2.

1. The House of Representatives shall be composed of members chosen every second year by the people of the several States: and the electors in each State shall be citizens of the Confederate States, and have the qualifications requisite for electors of the most numerous branch of the State Legislature; but no person of foreign birth, not a citizen of the Confederate States, shall be allowed to vote for any officer, civil or political, State or Federal.

2. No person shall be a Representative, who shall not have attained the age of twenty-five years, and be a citizen of the Confederate States, and who shall not, when elected, be an inhabitant of that State in which he shall be chosen.

3. Representatives and Direct Taxes shall be apportioned among the several States, which may be included within this Confederacy, according to their respective numbers, which shall be determined, by adding to the whole number of free persons.

including those bound to service for a term of years, and excluding Indians not taxed, three-fifths of all slaves. The actual enumeration shall be made within three years after the first meeting of the Congress of the Confederate States, and within every subsequent term of ten years, in such manner as they shall, by law, direct. The number of Representatives shall not exceed one for every fifty thousand, but each State shall have at least one Representative; and until such enumeration shall be made, the State of South Carolina shall be entitled to choose six—the State of Georgia ten—the State of Alabama nine—the State of Florida two—the State of Mississippi seven—the State of Louisiana six, and the State of Texas six.

4. When vacancies happen in the representation from any State, the Executive authority thereof shall issue writs of election to fill such vacancies.

5. The House of Representatives shall choose their Speaker and other officers; and shall have the sole power of impeachment; except that any judicial or other federal officer, resident and acting solely within the limits of any State, may be impeached by a vote of two-thirds of both branches of the Legislature thereof.

SECTION 3.

1. The Senate of the Confederate States shall be composed of two Senators from each State, chosen for six years by the Legislature thereof, at the regular session next immediately preceding the commencement of the term of service; and each Senator shall have one vote.

2. Immediately after they shall be assembled, in consequence of the first election, they shall be divided as equally as may be into three classes. The seats of the Senators of the first class shall be vacated at the expiration of the second year; of the second class at the expiration of the fourth year; and of the third class at the expiration of the sixth year; so that one-third may be chosen every second year; and if vacancies happen by resignation or otherwise, during the recess of the legislature of any State, the executive thereof may make temporary appointments until the next meeting of the Legislature, which shall then fill such vacancies.

3. No person shall be a Senator who shall not have attained the age of thirty years, and be a citizen of the Confederate States, and who shall not, when elected, be an inhabitant of the State for which he shall be chosen.

4. The Vice President of the Confederate States shall be President of the Senate, but shall have no vote, unless they be equally divided.

5. The Senate shall choose their other officers; and also a

President *pro tempore,* in the absence of the Vice President, or when he shall exercise the office of President of the Confederate States.

6. The Senate shall have the sole power to try all impeachments. When sitting for that purpose, they shall be on oath or affirmation. When the President of the Confederate States is tried, the Chief Justice shall preside; and no person shall be convicted without the concurrence of two-thirds of the members present.

7. Judgment in cases of impeachment shall not extend further than to removal from office, and disqualification to hold and enjoy any office of honor, trust or profit under the Confederate States; but the party convicted shall, nevertheless, be liable and subject to indictment, trial, judgment and punishment according to law.

SECTION 4.

1. The times, places and manner of holding elections for Senators and Representatives shall be prescribed in each State by the legislature thereof, subject to the provisions of this Constitution; but the Congress may, at any time, by law, make or alter such regulations, except as to the times and places of choosing Senators.

2. The Congress shall assemble at least once in every year: and such meeting shall be on the first Monday in December, unless they shall, by law, appoint a different day.

SECTION 5.

1. Each House shall be the judge of the elections, returns and qualifications of its own members, and a majority of each shall constitute a quorum to do business; but a smaller number may adjourn from day to day, and may be authorized to compel the attendance of absent members, in such manner and under such penalties as each House may provide.

2. Each House may determine the rules of its proceedings, punish its members for disorderly behavior, and with the concurrence of two-thirds of the whole number, expel a member.

3. Each House shall keep a journal of its proceedings, and from time to time publish the same, excepting such parts as may in their judgment require secrecy; and the yeas and nays of the members of either House, on any question, shall, at the desire of one-fifth of those present, be entered on the journal.

4. Neither House, during the session of Congress, shall, without the consent of the other, adjourn for more than three days, nor to any other place than that in which the two Houses shall be sitting.

Section 6.

1. The Senators and Representatives shall receive a compensation for their services, to be ascertained by law, and paid out of the treasury of the Confederate States. They shall in all cases, except treason, felony, and breach of the peace, be privileged from arrest during their attendance at the session of their respective Houses, and in going to and returning from the same; and for any speech or debate in either House, they shall not be questioned in any other place.

2. No Senator or Representative shall, during the time for which he was elected, be appointed to any civil office under the authority of the Confederate States, which shall have been created or the emoluments whereof shall have been increased during such time; and no person holding any office under the Confederate States shall be a member of either House during his continuance in office. But Congress may, by law, grant to the principal officer in each of the Executive Departments a seat upon the floor of either House, with the privilege of discussing any measures appertaining to his department.

Section 7.

1. All bills for raising revenue shall originate in the House of Representatives; but the Senate may propose or concur with amendments, as on other bills.

2. Every bill which shall have passed both Houses, shall, before it becomes a law, be presented to the President of the Confederate States; if he approve, he shall sign it; but if not, he shall return it with his objections to that House in which it shall have originated, who shall enter the objections at large on their journal, and proceed to reconsider it. If, after such reconsideration, two-thirds of that House shall agree to pass the bill, it shall be sent, together with the objections, to the other House. by which it shall likewise be reconsidered, and if approved by two-thirds of that House, it shall become a law. But in all such cases, the votes of both Houses shall be determined by yeas and nays, and the names of the persons voting for and against the bill shall be entered on the journal of each House respectively. If any bill shall not be returned by the President within ten days (Sundays excepted) after it shall have been presented to him, the same shall be a law, in like manner as if he had signed it, unless the Congress, by their adjournment, prevent its return, in which case it shall not be a law. The President may approve any appropriation and disapprove any other appropriation in the same bill. In such case he shall, in signing the bill designate the appropriations disapproved; and shall return a copy of such appropriations, with his objections, to the House in which the

bill shall have originated; and the same proceedings shall then be had as in case of other bills disapproved by the President.

3. Every order, resolution or vote, to which the concurrence of both Houses may be necessary (except on a question of adjournment) shall be presented to the President of the Confederate States; and before the same shall take effect, shall be approved by him; or being disapproved by him, shall be re-passed by two-thirds of both Houses according to the rules and limitations prescribed in case of a bill.

SECTION 8.

The Congress shall have power—

1. To lay and collect taxes, duties, imposts and excises for revenue necessary to pay the debts, provide for the common defence and carry on the government of the Confederate States: but no bounties shall be granted from the treasury; nor shall any duties or taxes on importations from foreign nations be laid to promote or foster any branch of industry; and all duties, imposts and excises shall be uniform throughout the Confederate States:

2. To borrow money on the credit of the Confederate States:

3. To regulate commerce with foreign nations, and among the several States, and with the Indian tribes; but neither this nor any other clause contained in the Constitution shall ever be construed to delegate the power to Congress to appropriate money for any internal improvement intended to facilitate commerce; except for the purpose of furnishing lights, beacons and buoys and other aids to navigation upon the coasts, and the improvement of harbors and removing of obstructions in river navigation, in all of which cases such duties shall be laid on the navigation facilitated thereby as may be necessary to pay the costs and expenses thereof:

4. To establish uniform laws of naturalization and uniform laws on the subject of bankruptcies throughout the Confederate States, but no law of Congress shall discharge any debt contracted before the passage of the same:

5. To coin money, regulate the value thereof and of foreign coin, and fix the standard of weights and measures:

6. To provide for the punishment of counterfeiting the securities and current coin of the Confederate States:

7. To establish post offices and post routes; but the expenses of the Post Office Department, after the first day of March in the year of our Lord eighteen hundred and sixty-three, shall be paid out of its own revenues:

8. To promote the progress of science and useful arts, by secu-

3

ring for limited times to authors and inventors, the exclusive right
to their respective writings and discoveries:

9. To constitute tribunals inferior to the Supreme Court:

10. To define and punish piracies and felonies committed on
the high seas and offences against the law of nations:

11. To declare war, grant letters of marque and reprisal, and
make rules concerning captures on land and water:

12. To raise and support armies; but no appropriation of money to that use shall be for a longer term than two years:

13. To provide and maintain a navy:

14. To make rules for the government and regulation of the
land and naval forces:

15. To provide for calling forth the militia to execute the laws
of the Confederate States, suppress insurrections and repel invasions:

16. To provide for organizing, arming and disciplining the militia, and for governing such part of them as may be employed in the service of the Confederate States; reserving to the
States, respectively, the appointment of the officers, and the authority of training the militia according to the discipline prescribed by Congress:

17. To exercise exclusive legislation, in all cases whatsoever,
over such district (not exceeding ten miles square) as may, by
cession of one or more States, and the acceptance of Congress, become the seat of the Government of the Confederate States; and
to exercise like authority over all places purchased by the consent
of the legislature of the State in which the same shall be, for the
erection of forts, magazines, arsenals, dockyards and other needful buildings: and

18. To make all laws which shall be necessary and proper for
carrying into execution the foregoing powers, and all other powers vested by this Constitution in the government of the Confederate States, or in any department or officer thereof.

Section 9.

1. The importation of negroes of the African race, from any
foreign country, other than the slaveholding States or Territories
of the United States of America, is hereby forbidden; and Congress is required to pass such laws as shall effectually prevent
the same.

2. Congress shall also have power to prohibit the introduction
of slaves from any State not a member of, or Territory not belonging to, this Confederacy.

3. The privilege of the writ of habeas corpus shall not be suspended, unless when in cases of rebellion or invasion the public
safety may require it.

4. No bill of attainder, or *post facto* law, or law denying or impairing the right of property in negro slaves shall be passed.

5. No capitation or other direct tax shall be laid, unless in proportion to the census or enumeration hereinbefore directed to be taken.

6. No tax or duty shall be laid on articles exported from any State, except by a vote of two-thirds of both Houses.

7. No preference shall be given by any regulation of commerce or revenue to the ports of one State over those of another.

8. No money shall be drawn from the Treasury, but in consequence of appropriations made by law ; and a regular statement and account of the receipts and expenditures of all public money shall be published from time to time.

9. Congress shall appropriate no money from the Treasury except by a vote of two-thirds of both Houses, taken by yeas and nays, unless it be asked and estimated for by some one of the heads of Department, and submitted to Congress by the President ; or for the purpose of paying its own expenses and contingencies ; or for the payment of claims against the Confederate States, the justice of which shall have been judicially declared by a tribunal for the investigation of claims against the government, which it is hereby made the duty of Congress to establish.

10. All bills appropriating money shall specify in federal currency the exact amount of each appropriation and the purposes for which it is made ; and Congress shall grant no extra compensation to any public contractor, officer, agent or servant, after such contract shall have been made or such service rendered.

11. No title of nobility shall be granted by the Confederate States ; and no person holding any office of profit or trust under them, shall, without the consent of Congress, accept of any present, emolument, office or title of any kind whatever from any king, prince or foreign State.

12. Congress shall make no law respecting an establishment of religion or prohibiting the free exercise thereof ; or abridging the freedom of speech, or of the press ; or the right of the people peaceably to assemble and petition the government for a redress of grievances.

13. A well regulated militia being necessary to the security of a free State, the right of the people to keep and bear arms shall not be infringed.

14. No soldier shall, in time of peace, be quartered in any house without the consent of the owner ; nor in time of war, but in a manner to be prescribed by law.

15. The right of the people to be secure in their persons, houses, papers and effects against unreasonable searches and seizures, shall not be violated ; and no warrant shall issue but

upon probable cause, supported by oath or affirmation, and particularly describing the place to be searched and the persons or things to be seized.

16. No person shall be held to answer for a capital or otherwise infamous crime, unless on a presentment or indictment of a grand jury, except in cases arising in the land or naval forces, or in the militia, when in actual service, in time of war or public danger; nor shall any person be subject for the same offence to be twice put in jeopardy of life or limb : nor be compelled, in any criminal case to be a witness against himself; nor be deprived of life, liberty, or property, without due process of law : nor shall private property be taken for public use, without just compensation.

17. In all criminal prosecutions the accused shall enjoy the right to a speedy and public trial, by an impartial jury of the State and district wherein the crime shall have been committed, which district shall have been previously ascertained by law, and to be informed of the nature and cause of the accusation; to be confronted with the witnesses against him : to have compulsory process for obtaining witnesses in his favor : and to have the assistance of counsel for his defence.

18. In suits at common law, where the value in controversy shall exceed twenty dollars, the right of trial by jury shall be preserved; and no fact so tried by a jury shall be otherwise reexamined in any court of the Confederacy than according to the rules of the common law.

19. Excessive bail shall not be required, nor excessive fines imposed, nor cruel and unusual punishments inflicted.

20. Every law or resolution having the force of law shall relate to but one subject, and that shall be expressed in the title.

SECTION 10.

1. No State shall enter into any treaty, alliance or confederation; grant letters of marque and reprisal; coin money; make anything but gold and silver coin a tender in payment of debts : pass any bill of attainder, or *ex post facto* law, or law impairing the obligation of contracts ; or grant any title of nobility.

2. No State shall, without the consent of Congress, lay any imposts or duties on imports or exports, except what may be absolutely necessary for executing its inspection laws; and the nett produce of all duties and imports, laid by any State on imports or exports, shall be for the use of the treasury of the Confederate States : and all such laws shall be subject to the revision and control of Congress.

3. No State shall, without the consent the Congress, lay any duty on tonnage, except on sea-going vessels, for the improvement of its rivers and harbors navigated by the said vessels : but

such duties shall not conflict with any treaties of the Confederate States with foreign nations; and any surplus revenue thus derived, shall, after making such improvement, be paid into the common treasury. Nor shall any State keep troops or ships of war in time of peace, enter into any agreement or compact with another State, or with a foreign power, or engage in war, unless actually invaded, or in such imminent danger as will not admit of delay. But when any river divides or flows through two or more States, they may enter into compacts with each other to improve the navigation thereof.

ARTICLE II.

Section 1.

1. The executive power shall be vested in a President of the Confederate States of America. He and the Vice President shall hold their offices for the term of six years; but the President shall not be re-eligible. The President and Vice President shall be elected as follows:

2. Each State shall appoint, in such manner as the legislature thereof may direct, a number of electors equal to the whole number of Senators and Representatives to which the State may be entitled in the Congress; but no Senator or Representative, or person holding an office of trust or profit under the Confederate States, shall be appointed an elector.

3. The electors shall meet in their respective States and vote by ballot for President and Vice President, one of whom, at least, shall not be an inhabitant of the same State with themselves; they shall name in their ballots the person voted for as President, and in distinct ballots the person voted for as Vice President, and they shall make distinct lists of all persons voted for as President, and of all persons voted for as Vice President, and the number of votes for each; which lists they shall sign and certify, and transmit, sealed, to the seat of the government of the Confederate States, directed to the President of the Senate; the President of the Senate shall, in the presence of the Senate and House of Representatives, open all the certificates, and the votes shall then be counted; the person having the greatest number of votes for President shall be the President, if such number be a majority of the whole number of electors appointed; and if no person have such majority, then, from the persons having the highest numbers, not exceeding three, on the list of those voted for as President, the House of Representatives shall choose immediately, by ballot, the President. But in choosing the President, the votes shall be taken by States, the representation from each State having one vote; a quorum for this purpose shall consist of a member or members from two-thirds of the States, and a majority of all the States shall be necessary to a

choice. And if the House of Representatives shall not choose a President, whenever the right of choice shall devolve upon them, before the fourth day of March next following, then the Vice President shall act as President, as in the case of the death, or other constitutional disability of the President.

4. The person having the greatest number of votes as Vice-President, shall be the Vice-President, if such number be a majority of the whole number of electors appointed; and if no person have a majority, then, from the two highest numbers on the list the Senate shall choose the Vice-President; a quorum for the purpose shall consist of two-thirds of the whole number of Senators, and a majority of the whole number shall be necessary to a choice.

5. But no person constitutionally ineligible to the office of President shall be eligible to that of Vice-President of the Confederate States.

6. The Congress may determine the time of choosing the electors, and the day on which they shall give their votes; which day shall be the same throughout the Confederate States.

7. No person except a natural-born citizen of the Confederate States, or a citizen thereof at the time of the adoption of this Constitution, or a citizen thereof born in the United States prior to the 20th December, 1860, shall be eligible to the office of President, neither shall any person be eligible to that office who shall not have attained the age of thirty-five years, and been fourteen years a resident within the limits of the Confederate States, as they may exist at the time of his election.

8. In case of the removal of the President from office, or of his death, resignation, or inability to discharge the powers and duties of the said office, the same shall devolve on the Vice-President; and the Congress may, by law, provide for the case of removal, death, resignation, or inability both of the President and Vice-President, declaring what officer shall then act as President, and such officer shall act accordingly until the disability be removed or a President shall be elected.

9. The President shall, at stated times, receive for his services a compensation, which shall neither be increased nor diminished during the period for which he shall have been elected: and he shall not receive within that period any other emolument from the Confederate States, or any of them.

10. Before he enters on the execution of his office, he shall take the following oath or affirmation:

" I do solemnly swear (or affirm) that I will faithfully execute the office of President of the Confederate States, and will to the best of my ability, preserve, protect and defend the constitution thereof."

Section 2.

1. The President shall be commander-in-chief of the army and navy of the Confederate States, and of the militia of the several States, when called into the actual service of the Confederate States; he may require the opinion, in writing, of the principal officer in each of the Executive Departments, upon any subject relating to the duties of their respective offices; and he shall have power to grant reprieves and pardons for offences against the Confederate States, except in cases of impeachment.

2. He shall have power, by and with the advice and consent of the Senate, to make treaties, provided two-thirds of the Senators present concur; and he shall nominate, and by and with the advice and consent of the Senate, shall appoint ambassadors, other public ministers and consuls, Judges of the Supreme Court, and all other officers of the Confederate States, whose appointments are not herein otherwise provided for, and which shall be established by law; but the Congress may, by law, vest the appointment of such inferior officers, as they think proper, in the President alone, in the courts of law or in the heads of Departments.

3. The principal officer in each of the Executive Departments, and all persons connected with the diplomatic service, may be removed from office at the pleasure of the President. All other civil officers of the Executive Department may be removed at any time by the President, or other appointing power, when their services are unnecessary, or for dishonesty, incapacity, inefficiency, misconduct, or neglect of duty; and when so removed, the removal shall be reported to the Senate, together with the reasons therefor.

4. The President shall have power to fill all vacancies that may happen during the recess of the Senate, by granting commissions which shall expire at the end of their next session; but no person rejected by the Senate shall be re-appointed to the same office during their ensuing recess.

Section 3.

1. The President shall, from time to time, give to the Congress information of the state of the Confederacy, and recommend to their consideration such measures as he shall judge necessary and expedient; he may, on extraordinary occasions, convene both Houses, or either of them; and in case of disagreement between them, with respect to the time of adjournment, he may adjourn them to such time as he shall think proper; he shall receive ambassadors and other public ministers; he shall take care that the laws be faithfully executed, and shall commission all the officers of the Confederate States.

Section 4.

1. The President, Vice President, and all civil officers of the Confederate States, shall be removed from office on impeachment for, and conviction of, treason, bribery, or other high crimes and misdemeanors.

ARTICLE III.

Section 1.

1. The judicial power of the Confederate States shall be vested in one Supreme Court, and in such Inferior Courts as the Congress may from time to time ordain and establish. The judges, both of the Supreme and Inferior Courts, shall hold their offices during good behavior, and shall, at stated times, receive for their services a compensation, which shall not be diminished during their continuance in office.

Section 2.

1. The judicial power shall extend to all cases arising under this Constitution, the laws of the Confederate States, and treaties made or which shall be made under their authority; to all cases affecting ambassadors, other public ministers and consuls; to all cases of admiralty and maritime jurisdiction; to controversies to which the Confederate States shall be a party; to controversies between two or more States; between a State and citizen of another State where the State is plaintiff; between citizens claiming lands under grants of different States; and between a State or the citizens thereof, and foreign States, citizens or subjects; but no State shall be sued by a citizen or subject of any foreign State.

2. In all cases affecting ambassadors, other public ministers, and consuls, and those in which a State shall be a party, the Supreme Court shall have original jurisdiction. In all the other cases before mentioned, the Supreme Court shall have appellate jurisdiction, both as to law and fact, with such exceptions, and under such regulations as the Congress shall make.

3. The trial of all crimes, except in cases of impeachment, shall be by jury, and such trial shall be held in the State where the said crimes shall have been committed; but when not committed within any State, the trial shall be at such place or places as the Congress may by law have directed.

Section 3.

1. Treason against the Confederate States shall consist only in levying war against them, or in adhering to their enemies, giving them aid and comfort. No person shall be convicted of treason unless on the testimony of two witnesses to the same overt act or on confession in open court.

2. The Congress shall have power to declare the punishment of treason, but no attainder of treason shall work corruption of blood, or forfeiture, except during the life of the person attainted.

ARTICLE IV.

Section 1.

1. Full faith and credit shall be given in each State to the public acts, records and judicial proceedings of every other State.—And the Congress may, by general laws, prescribe the manner in which such acts, records and proceedings shall be proved, and the effect thereof.

Section 2.

1. The citizens of each State shall be entitled to all the privileges and immunities of citizens in the several States, and shall have the right of transit and sojourn in any State of this Confederacy, with their slaves and other property: and the right of property in said slaves shall not be thereby impaired.

2. A person charged in any State with treason, felony, or other crime against the laws of such State, who shall flee from justice, and be found in another State, shall, on demand of the Executive authority of the State from which he fled, be delivered up, to be removed to the State having jurisdiction of the crime.

3. No slave or other person held to service or labor in any State or territory of the Confederate States, under the laws thereof, escaping or lawfully carried into another, shall, in consequence of any law or regulation therein, be discharged from such service or labor: but shall be delivered up on claim of the party to whom such slave belongs, or to whom such service or labor may be due.

Section 3.

1. Other States may be admitted into this Confederacy by a vote of two-thirds of the whole House of Representatives, and two-thirds of the Senate, the Senate voting by States; but no new State shall be formed or erected within the jurisdiction of any other State; nor any State be formed by the junction of two or more States, or parts of States, without the consent of the legislatures of the States concerned as well as of the Congress.

2. The Congress shall have power to dispose of and make all needful rules and regulations concerning the property of the Confederate States, including the lands thereof.

3. The Confederate States may acquire new territory; and Congress shall have power to legislate and provide governments for the inhabitants of all territory belonging to the Confederate States, lying without the limits of the several States; and may permit them, at such times, and in such manner as it may by law provide, to form States to be admitted into the Confederacy. In

all such territory, the institution of negro slavery, as it now exists in the Confederate States, shall be recognized and protected by Congress and by the territorial government: and the inhabitants of the several Confederate States and Territories shall have the right to take to such territory any slaves lawfully held by them in any of the States or Territories of the Confederate States.

4. The Confederate States shall guarantee to every State that now is or hereafter may become a member of this Confederacy, a republican form of government, and shall protect each of them against invasion ; and on application of the legislature (or of the Executive when the legislature is not in session) against domestic violence.

ARTICLE V.

SECTION 1.

1. Upon the demand of any three States, legally assembled in their several Conventions, the Congress shall summons a Convention of all the States, to take into consideration such amendments to the Constitution as the said States shall concur in suggesting at the time when the said demand is made; and should any of the proposed amendments to the Constitution be agreed on by the said Convention—voting by States—and the same be ratified by the legislatures of two-thirds of the several States, or by Conventions in two-thirds thereof—as the one or the other mode of ratification may be proposed by the general Convention —they shall thenceforward form a part of this Constitution. But no State shall, without its consent, be deprived of its equal representation in the Senate.

ARTICLE VI.

1. The Government established by this Constitution is the successor of the Provisional Government of the Confederate States of America, and all the laws passed by the latter shall continue in force until the same shall be repealed or modified ; and all the officers appointed by the same shall remain in office until their successors are appointed and qualified, or the offices abolished.

2. All debts contracted and engagements entered into before the adoption of this Constitution shall be as valid against the Confederate States, under this Constitution, as under the Provisional Government.

3. This Constitution, and the laws of the Confederate States, made in pursuance thereof, and all treaties made, or which shall be made under the authority of the Confederate States, shall be the supreme law of the land : and the judges in every State shall be bound thereby, anything in the Constitution or laws of any State to the contrary notwithstanding.

4. The Senators and representatives before mentioned, and the members of the several State legislatures, and all executive and judicial officers, both of the Confederate States and of the several States, shall be bound by oath or affirmation to support this Constitution; but no religious test shall ever be required as a qualification to any office or public trust under the Confederate States.

5. The enumeration, in the Constitution, of certain rights, shall not be construed to deny or disparage others retained by the people of the several States.

6. The powers not delegated to the Confederate States by the Constitution, nor prohibited by it to the States, are reserved to the States, respectively, or to the people thereof.

ARTICLE VII.

1. The ratification of the conventions of five States shall be sufficient for the establishment of this Constitution between the States so ratifying the same.

2. When five States shall have ratified this Constitution, in the manner before specified, the Congress, under the Provisional Constitution, shall prescribe the time for holding the election of President and Vice-President; and for the meeting of the Electoral College; and for counting the votes and inaugurating the President. They shall also prescribe the time for holding the first election of members of Congress under this Constitution, and the time for assembling the same. Until the assembling of such Congress, the Congress under the Provisional Constitution shall continue to exercise the legislative powers granted them, not extending beyond the time limited by the Constitution of the Provisional Government.

| No. 29. |

An Ordinance providing for the division of the State into Congressional and Electoral Districts.

1. *Be it ordained by the people of the State of Florida in Convention assembled,* That for the purpose of providing for the representation of this State in the Congress of the Confederate States, the State shall be and is hereby divided into two Congressional Districts, which division shall continue until the General Assembly otherwise provides. In each of said Districts there shall be elected, by the qualified voters thereof, one Representative in

said Congress, who shall have been an inhabitant of the District in which he is elected at least six months preceding the day of election.

2. *Be it further ordained*, That when any new apportionment of representation is made, under the provisions of the Constitution of the Confederate States, the General Assembly shall divide the State into as many Districts of contiguous territory as there may be representatives allotted to the State of Florida by such apportionment.

3. *Be it further ordained*, That all that part of the State lying East of the Suwannee River, shall constitute the first Congressional District, and the remaining portion of the State, not included in the limits before mentioned, shall constitute the second Congressional District.

4. *Be it further ordained*, That an election shall be held on the first Monday in October next for two members to represent the State of Florida in the Congress of the Confederate States, which election shall be governed by the laws which regulated the elections of members of Congress of the late United States, save as to the qualification of voters.

5. *Be it further ordained*, That for the purpose of choosing electors for President and Vice-President of the Confederate States of America, the State is divided into two electoral Districts, corresponding with the two Congressional Districts before provided for, as follows: The first Congressional District shall be the first electoral District; and the second Congressional District shall be the second electoral District; and one elector from each of said Districts, and two from the State at large, shall be elected by general ticket by the qualified voters, until the General Assembly shall otherwise provide.

Done in open Convention, April 23, 1861.

| No. 30. |

Be it ordained by the people of the State of Florida in Convention assembled, That until the Confederate States make provision for the military defence of the Ports of Apalachicola, St. Marks, Cedar Keys, Egmont Keys, St. Augustine, the mouth of St. Johns River, Fernandina, and such other ports as may be necessary, the Governor of this State be and he is hereby authorized to use such means as in his judgment may be necessary for the proper defence of the points indicated.

Passed in open Convention, April 22d, 1861.

[No. 31.]

Be it ordained by the people of the State of Florida in Convention assembled, That all persons holding office, either civil or military in this State, or who may hereafter be appointed or elected to any office, civil or military, be required, before they enter upon the duties of their respective offices, to take the following oath or affirmation:

I do swear (or affirm) that I am duly qualified, according to the Constitution of this State, to exercise the office to which I have been elected (or appointed,) and will, to the best of my abilities, discharge the duties thereof, and preserve, protect and defend the Constitution of this State and of the Confederate States of America.

Passed in open Convention, April 23d, 1861.

[No. 32.]

Be it ordained by the people of the State of Florida in Convention assembled, That the two first paragraphs of the ordinance numbered two, in the printed and published copy of ordinances which were adopted by the Convention on the 15th day of January, 1861, be repealed, and that the last paragraph of said ordinance be limited in its application to such money or property as was received by the officers of the late United States in this State, up to the 10th day of February, A. D., 1861.

Be it further ordained, That the ordinance numbered three of the said published ordinances, which was adopted in Convention on the 15th day of January, 1861, be repealed, and that all judicial proceedings and records therein mentioned be transferred and delivered to the District Court of the Confederate States for the District of Florida.

Be it further ordained, That the ordinance numbered seven, continuing the offices of the late United States, and making them offices in this State, and providing to retain the persons in office, who held the same, which ordinance was adopted in Convention on the 17th January, 1861, and the ordinance numbered eight of said published ordinances, which authorized the Governor to receive into the service of this State officers in the service of the United States who should resign from such service, which ordinance was adopted in Convention on the 17th January, 1861, and the ordinance numbered nine of said published ordinances, which provided for the abolition of useless offices formerly existing in this State under the Federal Government, which said ordinance was adopted in Convention on the 17th January, 1861: the ordinance numbered eleven of said published ordinances, which gives power to the General Assembly to declare who are citizens of this State, and provides for the punishment of such persons as shall hold office in this State under the United States, which ordinance was adopted on the 17th January, 1861; the ordinance numbered seventeen, creating an Admiralty Court at Key West, which was adopted on the 19th January, 1861; the ordinance numbered eighteen, of the published ordinances, providing for the carriage of the mails in this State and for other purposes, which said ordinance was adopted on the 19th January, 1861; the ordinance numbered nineteen of said published ordinances, which transfers to the Circuit Courts of this State jurisdiction over the subjects of jurisdiction formerly within the control of the late District Court of the United States, which said ordinances was adopted on the 19th January, 1861; the resolution adopted in Convention on the 18th January, 1861, directing the General Assembly to provide for the maintenance of the Light Houses, and the resolution adopted in Convention on the 17th January, 1861, giving instructions to the Delegates sent to represent this State in the Convention of Southern States at Montgomery be and the same are severally annulled and repealed.

Passed in open Convention April 24th, 1861.

| No. 33. |

An Ordinance relative to the Public Lands of this State.

1. *Be it ordained by the people of the State of Florida in Convention assembled,* That the State of Florida has jurisdiction over the public lands within her limits, and she now assumes the proprietary right therein, and will account for the same, subject to any claims the State of Florida may have against the late United States, through the Government of the Confederate States, in such manner as may be determined in a final adjustment of all rights and questions pending between said Confederate States and such Government as may represent the other States of the late Federal Union.

2. *Be it further ordained,* That it shall be the duty of the Register of State Lands to take the control and management of the

lands enuring to the State on and since the 10th day of January, 1861, and sell them under the same rules and regulations, according to law, as other lands under his control are now sold, except that titles to the same shall be made by patents issuing in the name of the State of Florida, signed by the Governor and countersigned by the Register, with an official seal attached, which seal said Register is hereby required to provide; and that, for this service, he shall be allowed an additional Clerk, with a salary of eight hundred dollars, until otherwise directed by the General Assembly.

3. *Be it further ordained*, That all the books, maps, plats and other documents, instruments and other property in the possession of the late Surveyor General of Florida, the several persons who were late Registers and Receivers, and the several Timber Agents of the late United States in the State of Florida, shall, upon being required by the Register of State Lands, as soon as may be after the passage of this ordinance, be transferred to and be kept by him in his office at the Capitol; and for the cost of such transfer he shall make out his account, which, being audited by the Comptroller of Public Accounts, shall, upon his warrant, be paid by the Treasurer of the State.

4. *Be it further ordained*, That the persons having in their possession the books, maps, plats and other documents, instruments and other property belonging to the offices of the late Surveyor General of Florida, the Receivers, Registers and Timber Agents of the late United States, are hereby required to transfer and deliver the same to the Register of State Lands upon his requisition; except that the Spanish Archives in the posssession of the late Surveyor General are hereby required to be transferred by the person in charge of the same to the Clerk of the Circuit Court of St. Johns county, to be kept by him as a part of the records of his office, until otherwise directed by the General Assembly of the State.

5. *Be it further ordained*, That the Register be required to appoint one suitable person in each of the judicial circuits of the State, (except the Middle Circuit) as salesman or receiver of these lands, whose duty it shall be on application for the purchase of land, upon a deposit of the purchase money for the same, to communicate to the Register the name of the party applying, the range, township and section of land, and amount of money deposited, upon the reception of which the Register shall issue a patent for the same in the name of the party purchasing. That said salesman or receiver shall at the end of each and every quarter make to the Register a fair return of all lands entered at his office, embracing the name of the purchaser, the amount of money paid, and the range, township and section of land. That such salesman or receiver shall respectively enter

into such bonds, in such amounts and with such securities as may be approved by the Judge or Solicitor of their respective Judicial Circuits, and shall receive for their services the sum of two and a half per cent. on all actual sales at their respective offices. The Register shall draw on the several salesmen or receivers respectively, at the end of each and every quarter, for all moneys in their offices and thereafter on warrant of the Register, the Treasurer of the State shall pay the above commission to the respective salesmen or receivers.

6. *Be it further ordained*, That the Register of State Lands be and he is hereby required to complete any unfinished work in the office of the Surveyor-General, and for this purpose to engage the services of some competent clerk, who for such service shall receive such pay as the said Register by and with the advice of the Governor, may think proper. which amount shall. upon his warrant, be paid by the Treasurer.

7. *Be it further ordained*, That all money received from the sales of said lands, shall at the end of each and every quarter be paid into the office of the Treasurer of the State, to be applied to such purposes as may be hereinafter directed by ordinance of this Convention.

8. *Be it further ordained*. That no military or bounty land warrant issued by the Government of the late United States shall. after the passage of this ordinance, be located upon any of the Public Lands of this State, unless due proof shall be made under oath, before the Register of State Lands, or some Judicial officer. that such land warrant was held by a citizen of this State on the tenth of January, 1861 ; but all such warrants so held, and so proved, may be located upon any of the public lands of the State. in the same manner, and under the same laws and regulations as they could have been under the government of the late United States.

9. *Be it further ordained*, That all monies now in the hands of the Receivers of the several Land Offices be paid over to the Treasurer of the State, and they and their sureties shall be held harmless against all damages which may be claimed by the late United States by reason of their compliance with the requirements of this ordinance.

10. *Be it further ordained*, That the State of Florida hereby assumes all arrearages due by this State to all officers and employees connected with the Surveyor General's Department. and the officers and employees of the several land offices within this State, for services rendered subsequent to the tenth day of of January, 1861, who have given bonds in conformity with the ordinances of this Convention, to be paid upon warrant of the Register of State Lands upon the Treasurer, and that they account with the Register of Public Lands in this State for all monies

which have come into their hands from sales of lands since the date of tenth of January, 1861.

11. *Be it further ordained,* That the State of Florida hereby assumes all arrearages due by the late government of the United States to all officers and employees connected with the Surveyor General's department, the several land offices and all timber agents within this State for services rendered prior to the tenth day of January, 1861, the correctness of the same and that it had never been paid having been first made under oath before the Register, or some Judicial officer, and the same shall be paid by the Treasurer of the State, from funds arising from the sales of the public lands, upon the warrant of the Comptroller of Public Accounts, said Comptroller having first audited the same.

12. *Be it further ordained,* That all laws and parts of laws of the late Government of the United States, respecting the sales and surveys of the public lands in this State, and all rules and regulations concerning the same, which were in force in this State on the tenth day of January, 1861, and which are not inconsistent with any of the ordinances passed by this Convention shall continue in full force in this State.

13. *Be it further ordained,* That the several land offices at St. Augustine, Tampa, Newnansville and Tallahassee, and the office of Surveyor-General of the State of Florida, under the late United States, be and the same are hereby abolished.

14. *Be it further ordained,* That the Register of State Lands be and he is hereby authorized to make all necessary arrangements and to take all proper measures to bring into market, by first offering the same at public auction, all lands included in the Military and Naval Reserves of the late United States, excepting so much as may be deemed necessary for the use, occupation and possession of such forts, dock-yards, navy-yards, and other public structures as may be ceded by this State to the Confederate States, which shall be determined by a joint commission of two Commissioners, to be agreed upon by the Governor of the State of Florida and the President of the Confederate States, and excepting further certain lands in Hillsborough and Escambia counties, hereinafter provided for. The times of such public auction to be determined by said Register, by and with the advice of the Governor. *Provided, nevertheless,* the minimum prices of such lands within six miles of any railroad line shall be two and a half dollars per acre, and of other lands one dollar and twenty-five cents per acre, and the necessary expenses of such public sales shall be paid out of the proceeds thereof, and the balance of money arising from the same shall be paid into the Treasury as and for the same purpose as from other lands. After these lands shall have been so offered, the lands remaining

4

unsold, shall be subject to entry at the minimum price above named. All other lands already surveyed are hereby rendered subject to entry at the same prices as under the late United States.

15. *Be it further ordained*, That in all cases of erroneous entries heretofore made, or which may hereafter be made, which were cancelled by the authorities of the late United States, or which may hereafter be cancelled by the Register of State Lands of this State, and the purchase money for which has not been refunded, the Treasurer is hereby authorized and required to refund the same out of the moneys received by him on account of the public lands, upon the certificate of said Register that such entry or entries have been cancelled.

16. *Be it further ordained*, That should the Register of State Lands, in the discharge of his official duties, require legal advice, the Attorney General of the State shall be and he is hereby instructed to give the same upon application of said Register.

17. *Be it further ordained*, That the Governor of the State of Florida be and he is hereby required, by issuing Patents in the name of the State of Florida, signed by the Governor and countersigned by the Register of State Lands, with his official seal attached, to perfect all titles to lands heretofore sold or granted by the late United States, (where such sales or grants have not heretofore been patented, and where the laws of the late United States and of this State pertaining thereto have been fully complied with,) and also to such as may hereafter be sold in the land office of this State.

18. *Be it further ordained*, That if, at any time hereafter it shall, in the opinion of the General Assembly, be to the best interest of the State to reduce the price of these lands, such reduction may be made by a vote of two-thirds of both houses of that body.

19. *Be it further ordained*, That all moneys arising from the sales of these lands shall be applied to the payment,—first, of debts hereinbefore assumed by the State, and of the salaries of the several Land Officers herein provided for and the necessary expenses pertaining to the discharge of their duties. Secondly, to the payment of such interest as may accrue on bonds about to be issued by the State of Florida, and for the final extinguishment of the debt created by said bonds; and if, thereafter, there should be a residue, it shall be applied,—first, to the payment of any Treasury Notes which may be issued by the State, and if said fund shall not have been thereby exhausted, it shall be then applied to the ordinary expenses of the State.

20. *Be it further ordained*, That the County Commissioners of Hillsborough county, and their successors in office, be and the same are hereby made and appointed Commissioners for the loca-

tion, survey and division into blocks and lots of a town site on the military reservation in the aforenamed county, at such point adjacent to the town of Tampa, and in such manner as may, in their judgment, promote to the best advantage the sales of the same. And the said Commissioners shall further subdivide into farms, so much of the remainder of said military reserve, as in their judgment may be conducive to the sale thereof to the best advantage, excepting such portion thereof as may have been heretofore selected by the Agents of this State, and designated by them as swamp and overflowed lands; and for this purpose said Commissioners shall have power to employ a competent Surveyor, and shall make to said Surveyor a reasonable compensation, the amount of which shall be signified under their signatures to the Comptroller of Public Accounts, upon whose warrant the same shall be paid by the Treasurer.

21. *Be it further ordained,* That so soon as the above surveys shall have been completed, and at as early a day as practicable, the aforenamed Commissioners,having first given notice by advertisement for one month in the public newspapers in Tampa, Tallahassee, Jacksonville and Savannah, (one at each place) shall offer the same at public auction to the highest bidder, having first fixed a minimum price thereto; and should any person have any buildings or private property on any of these lands, and said lands should, on the sale thereof, be knocked off to any person or persons other than the owners of such buildings or other private property, then the said Commissioners shall select three suitable persons to assess and fix a valuation to such property; and thereupon the party having before bid off said lot or lots of lands shall be required to pay to the owner thereof the aforesaid valuation, or yield his claim to said land to the next bidder below.

22. *Be it further ordained,* That upon application of the purchaser or purchasers of all such lands, with a certificate of said purchase from the said Commissioners, and upon payment of the amount due for the same to the Register of State Lands, said sales shall be recorded and patented to the same in the same manner as other public lands.

23. *Be it further ordained,* That should any of such lands, so surveyed and divided under the direction of said Commissioners, remain unsold at such public sale, the Commissioners are hereby empowered to manage and dispose of said lands by private or public sale, and at such times as they may deem best.

24. *Be it further ordained,* That the remaining lands of the aforesaid Military Reservation, after the above portions shall have been so disposed of, shall be open for entry in the same manner as other public lands.

25. *Be it further ordained,* That the County Commissioners of the County of Wakulla be and they are hereby made and

appointed Commissioners to dispose of certain lots and lands reserved by the late Government of the United States at St. Marks, and such Commissioners are hereby empowered to sell such lots and lands either at public outcry or at private sale, as in their judgment may be best for the interest of the State.

26. *Be it further ordained,* That upon the presentation of the certificates of such sale, over the signatures of said Commissioners, to the Register of State Lands, and payment to said Register of the purchase money for the same, said sales shall be recorded and patented in the same manner as other public lands.

27. *Be it further ordained,* That the Commissioners of the County of Escambia, and their successors in office, are hereby authorized to select three Commissioners (and to fill vacancies therein,) whose duty it shall be, after selection shall have been made as hereinafter provided of so much lands of the Naval Reserve as may be deemed necessary for the use, occupation and possession of the forts, dock-yards, navy-yards and other public structures in the vicinity of Pensacola, to affix a fair valuation as a minimum price to all lots in the towns of Woolsey and Warrington which may have been improved and not selected as above, and offer the same at such minimum price to the owners of such improvements: but should such owners not be willing to pay the same, then all such lots shall be sold as other lands hereinafter directed.

28. *Be it further ordained,* That said Commissioners shall have power to employ a competent Surveyor, to lay off into lots and farms, under their direction, so much and such of the remaining lands of said Naval Reserve as they may deem conducive to the best interest of the State, and to affix a minimum value to the same, and after having given notice for one month in a public newspaper, published in the several towns of Pensacola, Tallahassee, Mobile and Montgomery, for the public sale thereof, at such time or times as they may deem advisable, they shall offer the same at public auction to the highest bidder. And the purchaser or purchasers of said land, as well as of the lots named in the foregoing section shall receive patents for the same, in the same manner as is hereinbefore provided, in section 26. Said Commissioners shall allow to said Surveyor a reasonable compensation, to be approved by the Register of State Lands, and upon his warrant to be paid by the Treasurer.

29. *Be it further ordained,* That should any lands of said Reserve, so divided, remain unsold, the said Commissioners are hereby empowered to sell the same, in such manner and at such times as they may deem to the best interest of the State. But should there be in said Reserve any lands not so divided, then the same shall be disposed of in the same manner as lands in other reserves hereinbefore provided for.

30. *Be it further ordained,* That the Commissioners afore-named, as well at St. Marks as at Tampa and Escambia County, shall be allowed two and a half per cent. on their actual sales of all such lots and lands, said amount to be ascertained and audited by the Register of State Lands, which shall upon his warrant be paid by the Treasurer of the State.

31. *Be it further ordained,* That should the demand for lands in South Florida, at any time in the judgment of the Governor of this State, render it advisable to bring the same into market, then the Governor of the State shall, with the advice and consent of the Senate, have power to instruct and require the Register of State Lands to proceed to have the same surveyed in the same manner and under the same rules and regulations as public lands in this State have heretofore been surveyed under the Government of the late United States, and to place the same in market.

32. *Be it further ordained,* That should such surveys be ordered, the expenses for the same shall be provided for by the General Assembly of this State, out of any money in the Treasury of the State, not otherwise appropriated.

33. *Be it further ordained,* That all laws and parts of laws, and ordinances and parts of ordinances, now in force in this State and conflicting with this ordinance, be and the same are hereby repealed.

34. *Be it further ordained,* That the General Assembly of this State be and the same is hereby debarred and precluded from giving, granting, appropriating, or disposing of these lands in any manner whatever: *Provided, however,* After the Bonds and the interest which may have accrued thereon, as well as the Treasury notes issued by this State, shall have been paid, then the General Assembly shall have power to apply any balance arising from the sale of these lands to the ordinary expenses of the State Government.

35. *Be it further ordained,* That the Governor of this State be and he is hereby authorized to appoint one Commissioner to act in connection with a Commissioner to be appointed by the President of the Confederate States, to select such and so much of the public lands of this State as may by them be deemed necessary for the use, occupation and possession of such Forts, Dock Yards, Navy Yards and other structures, as may be ceded by this State to the Confederate States.

36. *Be it further ordained,* That no provision contained in any of the ordinance relative to the public lands of the late United States is intended to affect or in any wise be construed to the prejudice of the rights which the State of Florida has acquired to the swamp and overflowed lands, under and by virtue of any act of the Congress of the said United States, granting said lands

to this State, whether the same have been located and selected or not; and the Trustees of the same are hereby authorized and required to cause the swamp and overflowed lands to be located and selected from such lands as have not yet been surveyed and offered for sale, as soon as the unsurveyed lands shall have been surveyed.

Done in open Convention, April 26, 1861.

[No. 34.]

An ordinance to raise money for the immediate exigencies of the State, and for the payment of the public debt.

1 *Be it ordained by the people of the State of Florida in Convention assembled,* That the Governor be and he is hereby authorized to borrow the sum of five hundred thousand dollars, to be applied, first, to the debts of the State, and secondly, to such other purposes as the condition of the country may render necessary.

2 *Be it further ordained,* That the Treasurer of the State is hereby authorized and required, under the direction of the Governor, to cause to be issued coupon bonds, in sums of $25, $50, $100, $500, and $1,000, amounting in the aggregate to $500,000, to be signed by the Treasurer, and countersigned and registered by the Comptroller; and the said bonds shall be made payable at the expiration of twenty years from the first day of July next, and the interest thereon shall be paid semi-annually in the city of Charleston, at the rate of eight per cent. per annum.

3. *Be it further ordained,* That at the expiration of five years from the first day of July next, the State may pay up any portion of the bonds, upon giving three months previous public notice at the seat of government of the particular bonds to be paid, and the time and place of payment, and from and after the time so appointed no further interest shall be paid on said bonds.

4. *Be it further ordained,* That the revenue arising from the sale of the public lands, except the proceeds of the lands specifically set apart for Education and Internal Improvements, shall be primarily applied to the payment of the interest on the bonds enacted by this ordinance.

5. *Be it further ordained,* That in case the revenue arising from sales of the lands herein devoted to pay the interest on said bonds shall be likely to be insufficient therefor, the General As-

sembly shall levy a special tax to pay said interest; and any law
for such purpose shall be passed at such period of time as will
prevent any failure to pay said interest.

6. *Be it further ordained,* That any excess of revenue arising
from the sale of the lands above which may be necessary for
payment of interest on said bonds, shall be invested by the Treasurer from time to time, under the instructions of the Governor,
in some safe stock, to constitute a sinking fund for the ultimate
redemption of the bonds. And should such excess at any time be
insufficient to create the necessary sinking fund to redeem said
bonds at maturity, the General Assembly shall provide from the
revenue of the State for such deficiency; and should such excess
exceed the amount necessary for the sinking fund aforesaid, then
the balance shall be paid into the State Treasury.

7. *Be it further ordained,* That the Governor shall cause
books of subscription for said loan to be opened, under the
superintendance of Commissioners appointed by him, in such
places as he may think proper.

8. *Be it further ordained,* That the money subscribed to the
loan hereby authorized shall be paid to the Treasurer of the
State, who is authorized, under the direction of the Governor, to
designate responsible places of deposit in this State, and in such
other places as he may think proper.

9. *Be it further ordained,* That the Treasurer shall deliver to
the subscribers to said loan, bonds as aforesaid for such amount
of money as each may have subscribed and paid under the provisions of this ordinance.

10. *Be it further ordained,* That this is declared to be in lieu
and substitution of the act passed by the Legislature at its last
session for creating a loan of five hundred thousand dollars, approved the 14th February, 1861, and that said act of the Legislature be and the same is hereby repealed.

Passed in open Convention, April 21st, 1861.

| No. 35.]

*Be it ordained by the people of the State of Florida in Con-
vention assembled,* That so much of Ordinance No. 22, heretofore passed by this Convention, giving power to the Governor,
by and with the advice and consent of this Convention, to appoint
Delegates to represent this State in the Provisional Government
be and the same is hereby repealed.

Passed in open Convention April 26, 1861.

[No. 36.]

An Ordinance for the relief of Railroad Companies and the Collectors of Customs.

Be it ordained by the people of the State of Florida in Convention assembled, That all duties on importations of iron which were due to the Government of the late United States by the Pensacola and Georgia, and Alabama and Florida Railroad Companies, incorporated by the Legislature of this State, and any such duties which have become due by either of said Companies between the tenth day of January and tenth day of February of this year, may be secured to be paid by any of said companies by the execution of a bond, with two or more sufficient sureties, to be approved by the Treasurer of the State, in a penalty of double the amount of the duties due; which bond or bonds shall be made payable to the Governor, or his successors in office, twelve months after their date, with interest at the rate of eight per cent. per annum from the date at which such duties become due. And such bond or bonds shall be deposited with said Treasurer. And in case of failure of the payment of such sum or sums so secured to be paid, the Circuit Court of Leon County shall, on motion of the Attorney-General, award judgment and execution against the parties to said bond or bonds, written notice of the intention to make such motion having been served on each and every of said parties to said bonds ten days before the day on which such motion is to be made; and the execution on any judgment so rendered shall issue instanter; and a sale of property levied on under such execution shall take place on any day in the year, after notice shall have been given as provided by law in cases of sales under execution.

Be it further ordained, That upon the presentation to any Collector of a certificate from the Treasurer that bonds have been given as hereinbefore required, said Collector be and he is hereby authorized to deliver to the Company or their agent, any and all iron on which the duties were or are due as aforesaid, and to close his accounts with the Pensacola and Georgia, and the Alabama and Florida Railroad Companies for duties, and to return to them any assets which they may have placed in his hands as collateral security, the State assuming hereby all the responsibility that attached to said Collector on account of said duties.

Passed in open Convention, the 27th of April, 1861.

[No. 37.]

Be it ordained by the people of the State of Florida in Convention assembled, That the "qualified surrender of the Forts, munitions of war, &c., at Pensacola," made to the "Provisional Government of the Confederate States, by the Governor of this State" be and the same is hereby approved and confirmed.

Be it further ordained, That all Forts, Light Houses, Buoys, Dock Yards, Navy Yards, Arsenals, Barracks, Hospitals, and other public structures within the State of Florida, excepting the Arsenal on the Chattahoochee and the necessary lands around the same, the Barracks in St. Augustine and grounds attached, and such public buildings as may be on the Military Reserve at Tampa, together with so much of the lands around the same as may be selected by Commissioners appointed for that purpose, heretofore provided for by ordinance of this Convention, be and the same are hereby ceded to the Confederate States of America, for their occupation, use and possession for the common protection and benefit of said Confederate States so long as Florida shall be and continue a member of the same.

Be it further ordained, That the Legislature be empowered to dispose of the Arsenal at Chattahoochee, and the Barracks at St. Augustine, to such uses and purposes as in their judgment may seem best.

Passed in open Convention, April 27th, 1861.

| No. 38. |

An Ordinance for Military Purposes.

Be it ordained by the people of the State of Florida in Convention assembled, That whenever the protection of the people and defence of the State from sudden or apprehended invasion shall require, the Governor be and he is hereby authorized to call into service such number of troops as he may deem necessary for such purpose, and such troops, while in service, shall be subject to the rules and articles of war of the Confederate States, and he shall appoint the commanding officer of such force, with rank and pay to correspond with the number of troops called into service. The other commissioned officers shall be elected by the troops.

Be it further ordained, That the Governor shall have power to appoint and commission engineers and artillery officers, and such other officers as may be necessary, to instruct the troops and militia in military tactics, and to prescribe their rank.

Be it further ordained, That all staff officers shall be appointed from among the citizens, either civil or military, at the discretion of the appointing power, and that all laws and parts of laws conflicting with this ordinance be and the same are hereby repealed.

Be it further ordained, That the officers and men of all ranks and grades in the service of Florida, when called into service or placed on duty, shall receive the same pay as officers and men of like rank in the army of the Confederate States.

Be it further ordained, That the officers created by this ordinance for special service, shall vacate their commissions whenever the service for which they have been called shall have terminated and the men mustered out of service.

Be it further ordained, That the Governor shall have power to appoint the following staff officers: One Adjutant and Inspector-General, one Surgeon-General and four Aids-de-Camp, with the rank of Colonel; one Quartermaster-General, and one Paymaster-General, with the rank of Lieutenant-Colonel; and the said Quartermaster-General shall also perform the duties of Chief of Ordnance.

Be it further ordained, That the Surgeons and Assistant-Surgeons for all troops called into service shall be appointed and commissioned by the Governor.

Done in open Convention, April 27, 1861.

[No. 39.]

WHEREAS, A conflict of arms has happened between the forces of the Government holding possession of the army and navy of the late United States, and a war of invasion has been commenced by said Government upon the rights, liberties and soil of the people of the Confederate States, and as adhering to such Government, voluntarily admitting its authority and obeying its commands, assisting its military or naval operations against the Confederate States by any inhabitant or citizen of the State of Florida, would be justly punishable as a crime of the greatest magnitude, and whereas, the stirring up and promoting of rebellion and disaffection to the Government of the Confederate States, are at the present time acts dangerous to our safety as a people; therefore, for the purpose of detering all evil disposed persons from being guilty of such crime :

Be it ordained by the people of the State of Florida in Convention assembled, That if any person, being an inhabitant or citizen of this State, shall voluntarily and without force acknowledge and obey any laws or orders of the Government of the late United States of America, sought to be enforced in this State, or shall take or hold office under the authority thereof, or shall plead and practice as an attorney at law or solicitor in equity, or proctor in Admiralty, before any Court in this State claiming to act under the laws of said United States, the persons so offending, shall, upon conviction, be punished by fine and imprisonment, at the discretion of the jury, and shall moreover forfeit all of his or their lands, tenements, goods and chattels to the use of the State, and be forever disqualified from the privileges of citizenship in this State.

Be it further ordained, That if any person who resided in this State on the 10th day of January last, shall depart from the State after the passage of this ordinance for the purpose of acquiring a residence or becoming a citizen of any of the States of the late United States, which shall assist the Government at Washington, claiming to be the Government of the United States, against the Confederate States, the property of such person so taking refuge with the enemies of this State and of the Confederate States, shall be seized by the order of the Executive and confiscated by the judgment of the Circuit Court on proof of the acts aforesaid being made before said Court.

Be it further ordained, That if any person shall, by speech or writing, strive to stir up a rebellion in this State against the authority of the State or of the Confederate States, or shall, by word or deed, endeavor to create sedition or be engaged in any seditious or rebellious meeting assembled to excite resistance to the authority of this State, or of the Confederate States, or shall endeavor to seduce any one in the military or naval service of this State or of the Confederate States, to desert or betray a trust reposed in him or them, all persons so offending shall be guilty of Petty Treason, and on conviction shall be fined and imprisoned at the discretion of the jury, and be required to find security for good behavior, or in default, to remain in prison or be employed on any public work, as the Court may order.

Passed in open Convention, April 27th, 1861.

[No. 40.]

Be it ordained by the people of the State of Florida in Convention assembled, That the additional Section to the fifth Article of the Constitution adopted by the Convention on the 19th day of April, 1861, which is in the following words:

"The General Assembly shall have power to create special tribunals for the trial of offences committed by slaves, free negroes and mulattoes, and until the General Assembly otherwise provides, there is hereby created a Court in each County, which shall consist of two Justices of the Peace and twelve citizens, being slaveholders of the county, who shall have power to try all cases of felony committed in their county by slaves, free negroes and mulattoes, a majority of said Court may pronounce judgment, and all trials before it shall be upon the statement of the offence in the warrant of arrest and without presentment or indictment by a Grand Jury, the Sheriff of the county shall act as the ministerial officer of said Court, and the citizens who with the Justices are to compose the same, shall be selected by said Justices and summoned to attend by the Sheriff, and said Court shall assess the value of all slaves sentenced by it to capital punishment, one half of which value shall be paid by the State to the owner or owners of such slaves; and appeals from the judgment of said Court shall be had to the Circuit Court of the county upon an order made by the Judge thereof, upon an inspection of the record of the trial, full minutes of which shall be made by the said Justices, and such appeal, when allowed, shall operate as a *supersedeas*," be amended as follows: "Strike out the word "slaveholders," and insert "qualified jurors;" Strike out the following words from said section, "and said Court shall assess the value of all slaves sentenced by it to capital punishment, one half of which value shall be paid by the State to the owner or owners of such slave."

Passed in open Convention, April 27th, 1861.

| No. 41. |

AN ORDINANCE supplemental to an ordinance passed by this Convention April 26th, 1861, entitled "An ordinance to raise money for the exigencies of the State and for the payment of the public debt."

Be it ordained by the people of the State of Florida in Convention assembled, That the Register of Public Lands of this State be and he is hereby directed and instructed to receive in payment for any lands heretofore sold, or that may hereafter be sold through or by his office, nothing but gold or silver coin, or the bills of solvent banks, anything that may be contained in any act of the General Assembly to the contrary notwithstanding.

Be it further ordained, That the Register of Public Lands be and he is hereby required to give bond in the sum of thirty thousand dollars, with good and sufficient security, to be approved by the Governor of the State, for the faithful discharge of the duties of his office.

Be it further ordained, That the fractional townships of the public lands, lying along the boundary line between Florida and Georgia, shall be offered for sale in the same manner as is provided for by the ordinance for the sale of military and naval reserves, and in case any of the same shall not have been surveyed, it shall be the duty of the Register of Public Lands to cause the same to be surveyed.

Passed in open Convention. April 27th, 1861.

[No. 42.]

WHEREAS, Emergencies have rendered it necessary to call into service military organizations of this State, and to arm, equip, and transport the same; *and whereas,* the Governor has expended certain monies for said purpose:

Be it ordained by the people of the State of Florida in Convention assembled, That the Comptroller of Public Accounts be and he is hereby required to audit and allow all expenses incident to and arising from the same, heretofore made by Governor M. S. Perry.

Done in open Convention. April 27th, 1861.

[No. 43.]

Be it ordained by the people of the State of Florida in Convention assembled, That all persons now holding office in this State be continued in office until the term expires for which they were elected or appointed, unless sooner removed in the manner provided by the Constitution and laws of this State.

Done in open Convention, April 27th, 1861.

[No. 44.]

Be it ordained by the people of the State of Florida in Convention assembled, That the term of the Circuit Court of Walton county, held on the 12th day of March last, which Court was so held in place of the term as provided by law, to be held on the first Monday in March, be deemed and held valid, so far as civil cases are affected.

Passed in open Convention, April 27th, 1861.

[No. 45.]

WHEREAS, In consideration of a threatened invasion and the difficulty in the way of a speedy communication between the Capital and the Eastern and Southern sections of our State.

We, the people of the State of Florida in Convention assembled, do ordain, That the Governor be authorized to have constructed, without delay, a Telegraph Line along the Railroad to Baldwin, (where there is a centering of several telegraph lines,) on condition that the Railroad Companies along the route furnsih the posts and put up the line, the wire excepted.

Passed in open Convention, April 27th, 1861.

[No. 46.]

Be it ordained by the people of the State of Florida in Convention assembled, That the Governor of this State be and he is hereby authorized to cause any funds in the Treasury or in his control to be applied to equipping the forces called or to be called into service by the Confederate States.

Done in open Convention, April 27th, 1861.

RESOLUTIONS.

[No. 12.]

WHEREAS, It has pleased God to remove, by the hand of death, Dr. BENJAMIN W. SAXON, who was a member of this body, and who departed this life during the recess;

Resolved, That in testimony of our regard for the memory of the deceased and of our sympathy with his bereaved friends, we will wear the customary badge of mourning.

Resolved, That these proceedings be entered on the journal of this Convention, and that a copy of them be sent by the Secretary to the family of the deceased.

Done in open Convention, February 27th, 1861.

[No. 13.]

Resolved, That our Delegation to the Southern Congress be and they are hereby requested to bring the subject of the maintenance of Marine Hospitals, Light Houses, &c., within the State of Florida, to the attention of said Congress, and urge an immediate provision for the same.

Resolved, That the Secretary be required to dispatch a copy of the foregoing resolution to our Delegation.

Done in open Convention, March 1st, 1861.

[No. 14.]

Resolved, That this Convention do heartily and unanimously concur in the nomination and the election of the Hon. Jefferson Davis, President, and Hon. Alex. H. Stephens, Vice-President of the Confederate States.

Done in open Convention, March 1st, 1861.

| No. 15. |

Resolved, That the Governor be requested to communicate to this Convention whether any moneys have been paid out by any disbursing officer of the late Federal Government in this State, on any account, since the adoption of Ordinance No. 2, and if so, upon what account and upon what authority.

Done in open Convention, March 1st, 1861.

| No. 16. |

Resolved, That F. L. Dancy, late Surveyor-General in this State, be and he is hereby instructed by this Convention to retain possession of all papers and public documents and other public property appertaining to his office until he is further directed by this Convention.

Done in open Convention, March 1st, 1861.

| No. 17. |

Resolved, That this Convention now take a recess, to be re-assembled at the call of the President, or by the Governor, in the event of the inability of the President from illness or other cause.

Done in open Convention, March 1st, 1861.

| No. 18. |

Resolved, That the Committee on the Judiciary be instructed to inquire what action, if any, is necessary on the part of the Convention, to give effect to the act of the Provisional Congress of the Confederate States, creating a District Court for the State of Florida, and giving to said Court jurisdiction over the cases lately pending before the District Court for the Northern District of Florida.

Passed in open Convention, April 18th, 1861.

65

| No. 19. |

Resolved, That the duties of the Committee appointed to revise and digest the Constitution be so extended as to authorize and empower it to report such amendments thereto as it may deem proper.

Passed in open Convention, April 18th, 1861.

| No. 20. |

Resolved, That considering the embarassments that surround Governor John W. Ellis of North Carolina, at this time, that "tries the souls of men," the State of Florida is constrained to express her admiration for the decision and intrepidity of Governor Ellis, evinced by his indignant reply to the requisition made by the Black Republican President, and his prompt occupation of the Forts and Arsenals within a State that has not withdrawn formally from the late Federal Union.

Passed in open Convention, unanimously, April 19th, 1861.

| No. 21. |

Resolved, That the Secretary of this Convention be and he is hereby required to furnish a copy of the journal and proceedings of this Convention, and a copy of the Acts of the late General Assembly, to the University of Virginia, (of Albermarle County, Va.,) for the use of the Library of that Institution.

Done in open Convention, April 22d, 1861.

| No. 22. |

Resolved, That if necessary to have further assistance in bringing up the records of the Convention, the Secretary be authorized to employ the necessary assistance.

Done in open Convention, April 24th, 1861.

| No. 23. |

Resolved, That the Committee on Enrolments be instructed

3

to report to the Convention a list of such ordinances as are permanent and not subject to be repealed by the Legislature, and such as may be altered or repealed by such authority.

Passed in open Convention, April 26th, 1861.

[No. 24.]

Resolved, That the Attorney-General be requested to give to the Convention his opinion whether the accompanying proposed ordinance will, if passed, interfere with the vested right of any railroad company incorporated in the State—also whether there has been any decision of the Supreme Court made in any case in which the right of the Pensacola and Georgia Railroad Company to construct their line of road to any point on the boundary line of the State of Georgia, any if so, that he state what such decision has been, and annex to his opinion a copy thereof.

Passed the Convention April 26th, 1861.

[No. 25.]

Resolved, That the Committee on Enrolments be authorised to employ assistant Clerks to enrol the ordinances of the Convention.

Done in open Convention April 27th, 1861.

[No. 26.]

Resolved, That the Chief Secretary of this Convention be and he is hereby instructed to have printed 1000 copies of the amended constitution and the ordinances and resolutions passed by this Convention at its session on 26th of February, 1861, as well as its present session; that he cause 10 copies of the same to be sent to each member of the Convention, and 10 to the Clerks of the Circuit Courts of the several Counties of this State.

Done in open Convention, April 27th, 1861.

[No. 27.]

Resolved, That a Special Committee on Enrolment, to consist of three, be appointed to attend to the enrolment of all ordinances and resolutions passed by this Convention.

Done in open Convention, April 27th, 1861,

[No. 28.]

Resolved, That the Secretary of this Convention be authorized to audit the accounts of members, and that the same be paid by the Treasurer upon the warrant of the Comptroller.

Done in open Convention, April 27th, 1861.

[No. 29.]

Resolved, That while the people of the State of Florida heartily approve, in the main, of the Constitution of the Confederate States of America, and have given evidence of that approbation by the unanimous vote of this Convention on its ratification—yet there are certain parts thereof which, in the opinion of this Convention, should, at an early day, be amended; —with the view therefore of giving a proper expression of the sentiments of the people of this State, it is hereby suggested that the said Constitution would be greatly improved by the following amendments, to-wit :

That the *third* clause of the second section of the *first* article should be altered by striking out, after the word "determined" in the *fourth* line to the word "slaves," inclusive, and inserting the words "by the whole number of inhabitants within the State ;"

That the *first* clause of the *third* section of article *four* should be amended by inserting after the word "States," in the third line, the words "but no State shall be admitted into this Confederacy unless the institution of slavery shall be distinctly and clearly recognized in its Constitution and in actual operation under its laws," and by striking out the word "but" next following in the same line :

That the *seventh* clause of the *eighth* section of the *first* article should be amended by striking out the remainder of the clause after the word "routes," in the *first* line.

Passed in open Convention April 28th, 1861.

[No. 30.]

Resolved, That the President of this Convention, with three other members to be designated by him, be and they are hereby authorized to examine the enroled Constitution; and that after such examination the President be and he is authorized to sign the Constitution as enroled and approved.

Done in open Convention, April 27th, 1861.

[No. 31.]

Resolved, That in view of the increased and arduous labors performed by the Chief Secretary of this Convention during the present session, he shall be allowed six dollars per day for the same.

Done in open Convention, April 27th, 1861.

[No. 32.]

Resolved, That the thanks of this Convention are hereby tendered to the Hon. J. C. McGehee for the patient, unremitting and dignified manner in which he has presided over the present Convention.

Unanimously adopted in open Convention, April 27th, 1861.

[No. 33.]

Resolved, That this Convention now adjourn *sine die*, unless convened by the President on or before the 25th of December next.

Adopted in open Convention, April 27th, 1861.

TALLAHASSEE, May 4th, 1861.

I do hereby certify that the foregoing are true and correct copies of the ordinances and resolutions adopted in Convention at the called sessions of said body.

WILLIAM S. HARRIS,
Secretary of the Convention.